The Interpretation of Graphs in Physics

The Interpretation of Graphs in Physics

I S MacPherson, B Sc, Ph D, M Inst P
and
B R Jones, B Sc, M Sc, M Inst P
Lecturers in Physics at Farnborough Technical College

HUTCHINSON EDUCATIONAL

Hutchinson Educational Ltd
3 Fitzroy Square, London W1

London Melbourne Sydney Auckland
Wellington Johannesburg Cape Town
and agencies throughout the world

First published 1974

© I. S. MacPherson and B. R. Jones 1974
© Drawings Hutchinson Publishing Group 1974

*Printed in Great Britain by Anchor Press
and bound by Wm. Brendon,
both of Tiptree, Essex*

ISBN 0 09 116751 5

Contents

The Theory of Graphs	7
Hints on Plotting Graphs	29
The Assessment of Experimental Errors	36
The Experimental Tests	44
Answers, Comments and Graphs	91

Chapter 1   The Theory of Graphs

Aims of the book

Although this book has been written primarily to prepare physics students for paper 3 (part II) of the new University of London GCE Advanced level examination, the authors feel that it will fill a need in the teaching of physics at Advanced level standard for both Advanced level and OND students, possibly for ONC students as well. We have been dissatisfied for some time with the unsatisfactory way in which students acquire their knowledge of graph drawing and interpretation in a piecemeal fashion during practical work sessions. We have found that the weaker students in particular often have large gaps in their knowledge of experimental data techniques which the existing laboratory manuals with their very condensed theory sections do not fill. It seems to us that this is the situation which the University of London GCE examiners intended to rectify when devising the new syllabus (first examined in June 1973). Trials from Spring 1972 onwards at Farnborough Technical College have shown that the students acquire skills, even from only the first few tests, which they can and do apply to their laboratory work.

Nature of the tests

The first three chapters of the book cover the theory of graphs (including log-log and log-linear), the various techniques of drawing graphs and the assessment of experimental error. These give all the information needed to do the tests which follow in Chapter Four.

The early tests are simple laboratory situations in which the student is presented with a set of results, plots them, and then makes deductions from the graph. Some questions concerning the skill of the experimenter are occasionally included. The later tests involve more difficult plotting, choice of variables and deductions. Questions on the validity of the theory in view of the trends of the experimental results are asked and suggestions for further testing of the theory invited. The last four tests are of a non standard type and involve real life as opposed to Advanced level laboratory situations. The student should now have enough data handling skill not to be frightened by such tests and should also have enough background knowledge to make valid statements as to the practicability and accuracy of the proposed devices.

Fairly obviously in these later tests many of the answers are open to argument and our answers in the Appendix should not be regarded as the last word on the subject. We would in fact welcome comments from teachers and students on the tests in general and on any answers with which they may disagree.

Using the book

There are probably as many ways of doing this as there are teachers involved. We feel, however, that we can offer some suggestions from our experience, gained from the trials carried out at Farnborough Technical College.

Too early a start on the book would seem unwise. We would suggest a start in the middle of the second term of a six-term course to give the students time to settle down and acquire a little scientific self-confidence. The teacher should work through Chapters One and Two in class but omit the section on log graphs. This is best covered just before such graphs are first met in Tests 5 and 6. Chapter Three on experimental error can be worked through at any convenient time but we feel that it is best left until the second year of the course and that only the significant figures concept should be emphasised in the early stages.

We have found that the first few tests require close supervision in order to persuade the students into the correct methods of working. It would not be advisable to set these tests as homework or expect them to be completed at home. From Test 6 onwards, the students require less help with the graphical techniques and we have found that when these tests are completed without supervision satisfactory results are produced. In fact the whole of the weekly class period can be usefully spent on first individual, and then general discussion of the results of the previous test.

A time allowance of one hour per week over four and a half terms would seem at the moment to be required to cover the introductory chapters and the tests. The tests are a sequence and we feel that they should be done, as far as possible, in order even if lack of time forces some omissions. Although the test in the Advanced level examination will have a time limit of one and a half hours we have not specified target times for any of our tests. The early ones will probably take about one and a half hours since the students will be unfamiliar with the approach. We would expect a fall in this time due to increasing skill up to about Test 10. From there on the tests get longer and also more difficult so that students of different ability will now show widely different performances. It is very unlikely that any of the real life situation tests could be done adequately in less than one and a half hours.

Introduction

In experimental physics we are frequently concerned with the situation in which there are several variable quantities. For example the factors which affect the behaviour of a given mass of ideal gas are the pressure p, the volume V and the temperature T and they are related by the ideal gas equation,

$$pV/T = \text{constant}$$

If we wish to see how the pressure affects the volume then we have to hold the temperature constant. This leads to Boyle's law,

$$pV = \text{constant}$$

Similarly to see how the temperature affects the volume we have to hold the pressure constant, and to see how the pressure varies with temperature we must hold the volume constant.

Proportionality

We have just considered a specific example of the general approach in physics, which is that when we do experimental work we are almost always concerned with finding out how one quantity varies when another quantity is changed, the other possible variables being kept constant.

If we pass a current through a resistor which is held at constant temperature and measure the potential difference across it we find that increasing the current produces a corresponding increase in the potential difference. If the current is doubled we find that the potential difference is doubled, if the current is trebled we find the potential difference is trebled and so on. With such a variation the potential difference V is said to be directly proportional to the current I. That is,

$$V \propto I$$

Clearly V is not equal to I since V and I are different physical quantities but V is related to I by a constant factor, the constant of proportionality, which is called the resistance R of the resistor. Therefore

$$V = RI$$

It is found experimentally that R is temperature dependent but by holding the temperature constant we have made R a constant in the above equation and found out the relationship between the other two variables V and I as explained in the introduction.

We can now consider a slightly more difficult case where a quantity may be directly proportional to the power or root of another quantity. This may be illustrated by considering the motion of a water jet issuing horizontally from a pipe with a velocity v and acted upon by gravity. A simple diagram is shown in Fig. 1.1.

When v is low enough for the effects of air resistance to be ignored, theory shows that the path of the water jet is described by,

$$y = \left(\frac{g}{2v^2}\right)x^2$$

where x and y are respectively the distances measured horizontally and vertically from the open end of the pipe, and g is the acceleration due to gravity.

As g and v are constants we say that y is directly proportional to x^2. That is,

$$y \propto x^2$$

and the constant of proportionality is $(g/2v^2)$.

Another example where a power or root of a quantity is involved is in the formula for the fundamental frequency f_0 of a plucked sonometer wire. If a sonometer wire of length l, under a tension T and of mass per unit length m, is plucked its fundamental frequency is given by,

$$f_0 = \frac{1}{2l}\sqrt{\frac{T}{m}}$$

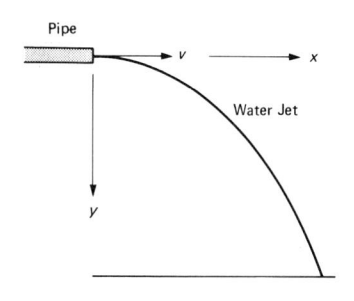

Fig. 1.1 The Water Jet.

Provided the tension of the given wire is kept constant then f_0 is directly proportional to $1/l$ or inversely proportional to l. That is,

$$f_0 \propto \frac{1}{l} \quad \text{or} \quad f_0 \propto l^{-1}$$

and the constant of proportionality is

$$\frac{1}{2}\sqrt{\frac{T}{m}}$$

An experiment could have been carried out in which the length was kept constant and the tension varied, in which case we would have found,

$$f_0 \propto \sqrt{T}$$

with the constant of proportionality being

$$\frac{1}{2l\sqrt{m}}$$

As an exercise try to think of at least four equations from other branches of physics which illustrate the direct proportionality between quantities. In particular try to find some which involve powers or roots of measured quantities. You should be able to obtain the respective constants of proportionality and these can be checked with your teacher or lecturer.

Reasons for using graphs

You will find that generally a graph is a very simple and convenient way of examining a series of experimental results. It is a visual display of the dependence of one variable quantity on another. When you plot a set of results you will be able to obtain a great deal of information about the dependence of the variables on each other very easily and quickly. You could obtain this information from a mathematical analysis of the results but you would find this both time consuming and laborious.

The advantages of treating results graphically can be illustrated by considering the experimental results listed in Table 1.1.

These results, which were taken during an experiment to measure the viscosity of a liquid, are of the terminal velocities v_t reached by spheres of different diameters d falling in a viscous liquid contained in a tube. Theory shows that provided the diameter of the sphere is small compared with the tube diameter,

$$d^2 \propto v_t$$

The diameter of the tube used in this experiment was 46 mm

The graph showing d^2 plotted against v_t is shown in Fig. 1.2.

Several important features are illustrated in this graph and each of these will now be considered.

(Sphere Diameter)^2 d^2, (mm^2)	Terminal velocity v_t, (mm s^{-1})
2·4	9·5
5·7	20·8
10·9	35·0
16·9	50·3
21·0	55·0
22·7	71·0
28·5	85·0
40·3	114·3
83·3	176·7

Table 1.1.

Linearity

Up to the point (22·5, 70) the graph is a straight line. This indicates direct proportionality between d^2 and v_t.

Fig. 1.2 Graph of (Sphere Diameter)² against Terminal Velocity.

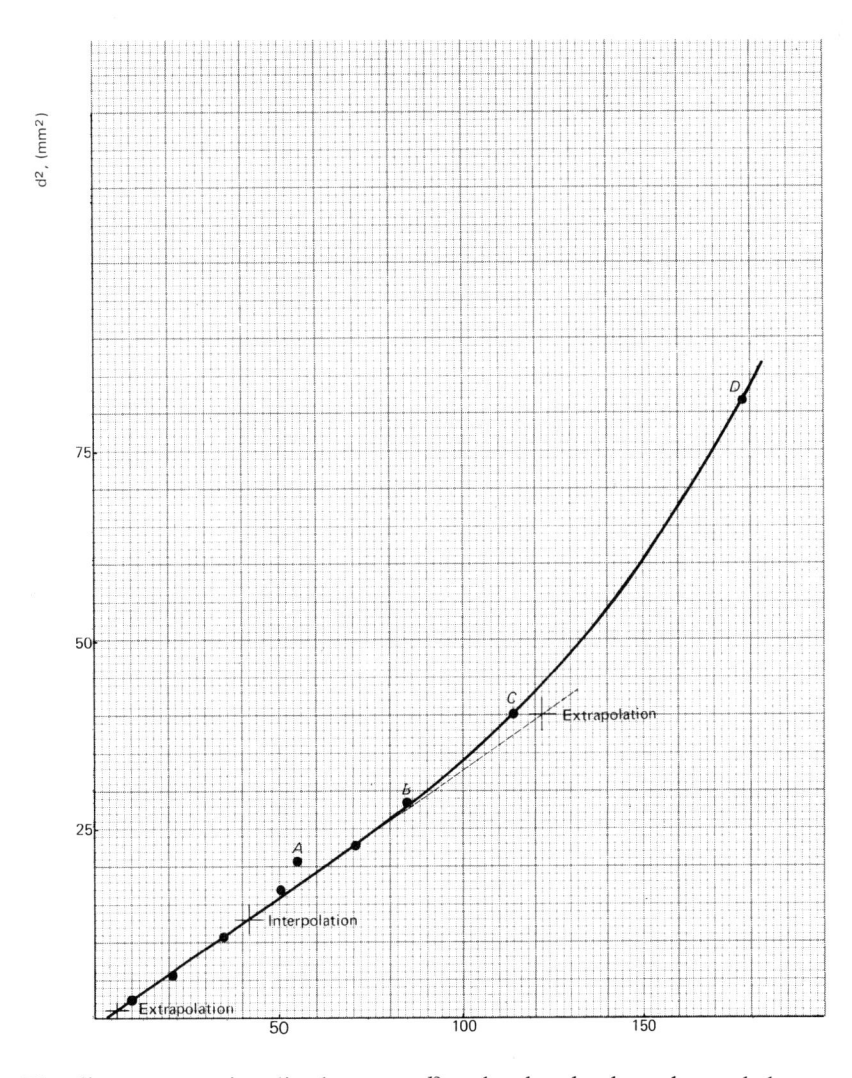

Non-linearity

The direct proportionality between d^2 and v_t breaks down beyond the point (22·5, 70). From this point onwards the graph is no longer a straight line and the simple relationship $d^2 \propto v_t$ no longer holds. This information could have been obtained from a careful study of the table of results but the graph makes this obvious.

Scatter

You will notice that there is a slight scatter of the points about the linear portion of the graph, and this can give a feeling for the size of the random errors in the experiment (mainly errors in timing leading to errors in v_t in this case). A section dealing with experimental errors is included later.

'Doubtful' points

You will notice that the point A on the graph was ignored when the ine was drawn because its distance from the line is several times that of any of the others and it can be considered a 'doubtful' point. Such points usually arise as a result of mis-reading during the experiment or by mis-plotting the result. There are no hard and fast rules about what constitutes a doubtful point, but a graph will show up such points and enable the results to be re-taken or the plotting to be checked.

A word of warning here. Doubtful points must not be omitted from the plot, particularly when they come at the extreme of the range of measurements as they may indicate a genuine change of behaviour. For example, on the graph *B*, *C* and *D* are genuine points which do not lie on the straight line.

Interpolation

An advantage of a graph is that it makes it very easy for estimations to be made between the actual measured results. This process is called interpolation and we can consider an example of this from the graph. We can see that the terminal velocity of a 3·6 mm diameter sphere ($d^2 = 13$ mm^2) would be 41·5 mm s^{-1} even though a sphere of this diameter was not used in the experiment. As an exercise write down the terminal velocity of a sphere of diameter 7 mm.

Extrapolation

Extrapolation enables us to make estimations beyond the range of the measured values. We can read off the terminal velocity of a 1 mm diameter sphere ($d^2 = 1$ mm^2) as 5·7 mm s^{-1} at the lower end of the straight line.

At times however extrapolation can be dangerous and unjustifiable. If the measurements giving points *B*, *C* and *D* had not been taken, then by extrapolating the straight line portion of the graph a sphere of diameter 6·35 mm ($d^2 = 40·3$ mm^2) would appear to have a terminal velocity of 122 mm s^{-1}. However the non-linear variation between d^2 and v_t in this region leads to a value for the terminal velocity of 114·3 mm s^{-1}.

There is even less justification in extrapolating a curve rather than a straight line beyond the range of the measured results since the curve is much more difficult to draw and an additional error is thereby introduced.

Straight line graphs

When we have an equation relating two variables it is generally possible to choose our variables in such a form that a straight line graph is obtained.

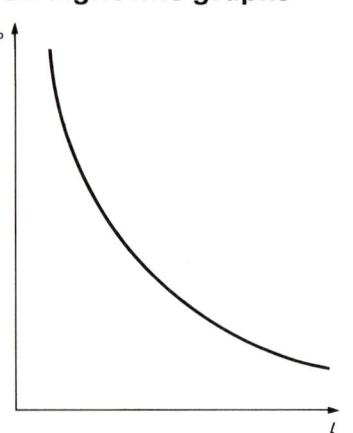

If we consider the equation for the fundamental frequency of a stretched string and plot f_0 against l we obtain the graph shown in Fig. 1.3. This graph is a curve (called a rectangular hyperbola) and no useful information can be easily obtained from it. However if we had chosen the form of our variables correctly as f_0 and $1/l$ and plotted them they give a straight line graph as shown in Fig. 1.4. In this case the graph can be used to give useful information. The slope of the graph is the constant of proportionality relating the two variables. That is

$$\frac{1}{2}\sqrt{\frac{T}{m}}$$

Fig. 1.3 Fundamental frequency (f_0) against length (l) for a stretched string.

The question arises here of how to draw the best straight line through the experimental points. This is discussed in detail later.

y = mx

If a variable y is directly proportional to another variable x then theoretically,

$$y = mx$$

where the constant of proportionality m is the slope of the graph when y is plotted as the ordinate (y axis) and x the abscissa (x axis). The slope is measured as,

$$\frac{\text{Increment in } y}{\text{Corresponding increment in } x}$$

or

$$m = \frac{\Delta y \text{ (measured in the units of the } y \text{ scale)}}{\Delta x \text{ (measured in the units of the } x \text{ scale)}}$$

Do not confuse the slope m with the tangent of the angle θ (see Fig. 1.5) that the straight line makes with the x axis, because the value of θ depends upon the choice of your scales. For example if the y scale were doubled then the tangent of the angle θ would double also but the slope m would not be affected.

Theoretically the line represented by the equation $y = mx$ should pass through the origin, $(0, 0)$, since when $y = 0$, $x = 0$ also. This is shown by the line OA in Fig. 1.5. In practice an experimental line may not pass through the origin, and this can be due to a consistent (systematic) error in either x or y so that all the values of x or y are wrong by the same amount. This does not affect the value of the slope m which is the main interest in graphs of this type.

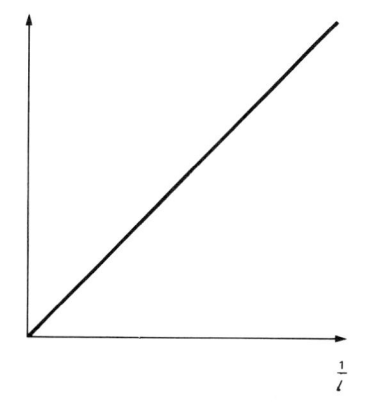

Fig. 1.4 Fundamental frequency (f_0) against length^{-1} ($1/l$) for a stretched string.

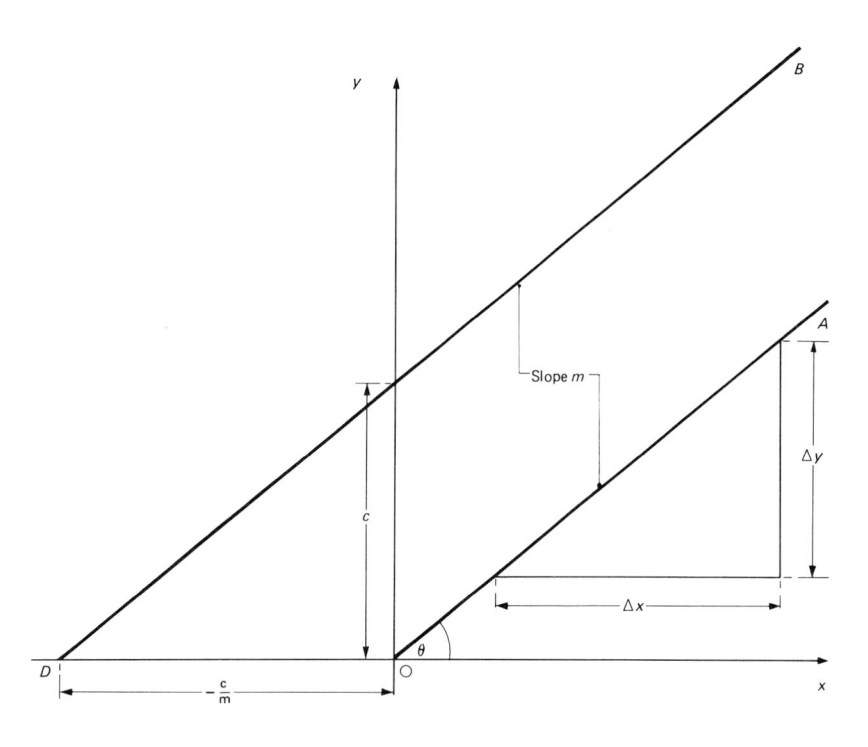

Fig. 1.5 Graph showing $y = mx$ (line OA) and $y = mx + c$ (line DB).

y = mx+c

There is another type of straight line graph where y is not simply proportional to x. If we consider line DB in Fig. 1.5 this is a straight line having the same slope m as line OA but it does not pass through the origin. It is represented by the equation,

$$y = mx + c$$

where c is the intercept on the y axis. An intercept is the distance from the origin to the point where the line, or a curve, cuts an axis.

If we consider what happens when line DB cuts the y axis (the equation of the y axis is $x = 0$) where $x = 0$ we have $y = 0 + c$. Hence c is the intercept on the y axis.

The line DB also cuts the x axis (the equation of the x axis is $y = 0$) and the intercept on the x axis can be obtained in a similar way, by substituting $y = 0$ into the equation. That is,

$$0 = mx + c$$

Therefore $x = -c/m$ is the intercept on the x axis.

The value for the intercept on the x axis could also have been obtained from the equation, (see Fig. 1.5),

$$\text{slope } m = \frac{c}{\text{intercept on the } x \text{ axis}}$$

Note that the intercept on the x axis is negative so that agreement with the above value $-c/m$ is obtained.

The general equation of a straight line is represented by,

$$y = mx + c$$

and this can be written,

$$(y - c) = mx$$

so that,

$$(y - c) \propto x$$

Note that if $c = 0$ we have the equation for a straight line passing through the origin.

As an example of the general equation for a straight line we will consider the formula for the variation of resistance with temperature,

$$R_t = R_0(1 + \alpha t)$$

where R_t is the resistance at the temperature t measured in degrees Celsius. R_0 is the resistance at 0°C and α is the temperature coefficient of resistance. The variables in this equation are R_t and t. α and R_0 are constants.

The first step is to rewrite the equation in the form of $y = mx + c$. This gives us,

$$R_t = (R_0 \alpha) t + R_0$$

When R_t is plotted as the ordinate and t as the abscissa we obtain a straight line graph having a slope of $R_0 \alpha$ and an intercept of R_0 on the R_t axis. By measuring the slope of the line and the intercept we can

Resistance R_t, (Ω)	Temperature t, (°C)
5·35	31
5·55	41
5·71	51
5·90	61
6·07	71
6·28	81
6·44	91

Table 1.2.

Fig. 1.6 Graph showing Resistance against Temperature.

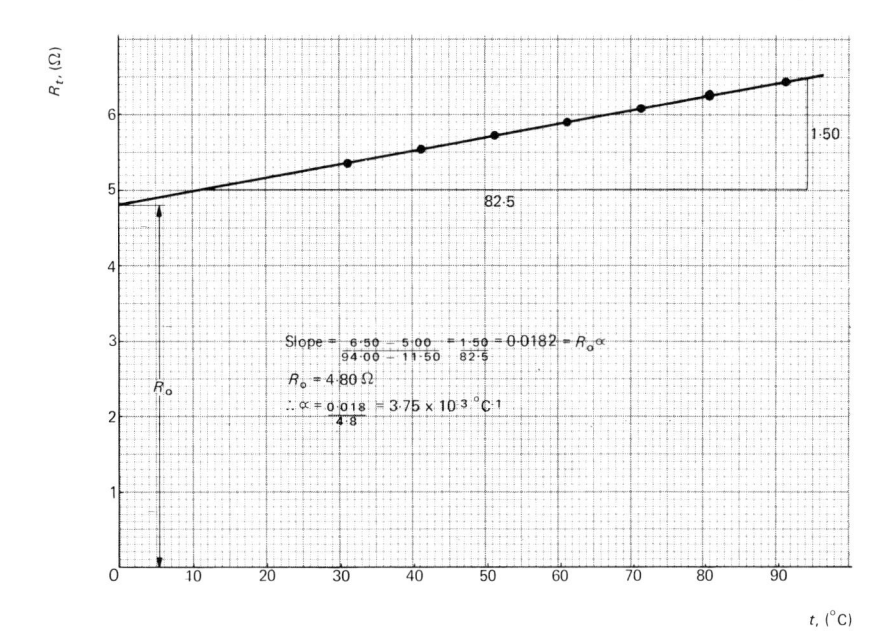

$$\text{Slope} = \frac{6\cdot50 - 5\cdot00}{94\cdot00 - 11\cdot50} = \frac{1\cdot50}{82\cdot5} = 0\cdot0182 = R_0\alpha$$

$$R_0 = 4\cdot80\ \Omega$$

$$\therefore \alpha = \frac{0\cdot018}{4\cdot8} = 3\cdot75 \times 10^{-3}\ °C^{-1}$$

calculate a value for α. Results for the variation of the resistance of a copper coil with temperature are shown in Table 1.2 and plotted in Fig. 1.6. The slope and the intercept have been measured as illustrated and α has been calculated to have a value of $3\cdot79 \times 10^{-3}\ °C^{-1}$.

You may have realised that there is an alternative method for calculating α which involves the intercept on the t axis. If we substitute $R_t = 0$ in the equation

$$R_t = (R_0\alpha)\,t + R_0$$

we have,

$$R_t = 0 = R_0\alpha t + R_0$$

$$\therefore t = -1/\alpha$$

This method has not been shown on the graph in Fig. 1.6 due to lack of space, but is illustrated in Fig. 1.7.

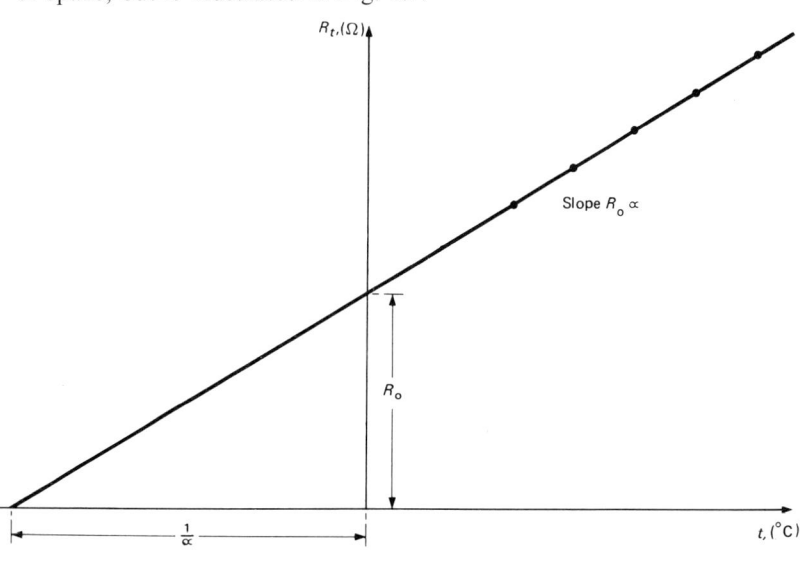

Fig. 1.7 Resistance against Temperature illustrating intercept on t axis.

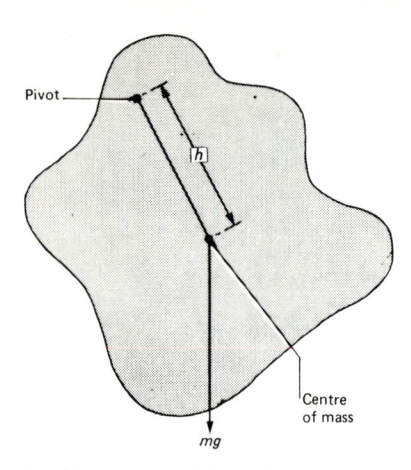

Fig. 1.8 Compound Pendulum.

Another example which is less obvious than the one just considered arises when we deal with the formula for the period of a compound pendulum,

$$T = 2\pi \sqrt{\frac{k^2+h^2}{gh}}$$

where k is a constant depending on the geometry of the pendulum, h is the distance between the pivot and the centre of mass (see Fig. 1.8) and g is the acceleration due to gravity. Squaring both sides of the equation we obtain,

$$T^2 = \frac{4\pi^2 k^2}{gh} + \frac{4\pi^2 h}{g}$$

We cannot use this equation in its present form to obtain a straight line graph since h appears in different ways in each of the terms on the right hand side of the equation. However if we multiply both sides of the equation by h we obtain,

$$hT^2 = \frac{4\pi^2 k^2}{g} + \frac{4\pi^2 h^2}{g}$$

which does have the form $y = mx+c$. If we plot hT^2 as ordinate and h^2 as abscissa we obtain a straight line of slope

$$\frac{4\pi^2}{g}$$

and an intercept on the hT^2 axis of

$$\frac{4\pi^2 k^2}{g}$$

False origins

If a true origin of axes is used ($x = 0$, $y = 0$) as in the graph in Fig. 1.6 the intercepts obtained are true ones. However since the measurements are bunched together in the y direction at a considerable distance from the true origin it is difficult to judge the best straight line. This may lead to an error in the slope which may only be small, but will lead to a considerable error in the intercepts. Generally you will find it an advantage to spread the points over the whole of the graph paper, by a suitable choice of scales even at the cost of not having a true origin.

The results for the variation of the resistance of the copper coil with temperature are shown in Fig. 1.9 where they have been spread over the graph paper by expansion of the y scale. Note that the true origin has not been shown and that the coordinates of the false origin are (5·0, 30). The intercept EF of this graph on the R_t axis is 5·34 Ω. It is clearly not the true value of 4·80 Ω obtained when using a true origin. How then can we obtain the true intercept value of 4·80 Ω using the false origin graph of Fig. 1.9? We will first of all consider the general case and then apply it to this particular problem.

Intercept calculation with false origins

We first measure the slope of the graph m (which is independent of the choice of origin) and then read off the coordinates $(\bar{x}, \bar{y})$ of any

Fig. 1.9 Graph showing Resistance against Temperature with Resistance scale expanded.

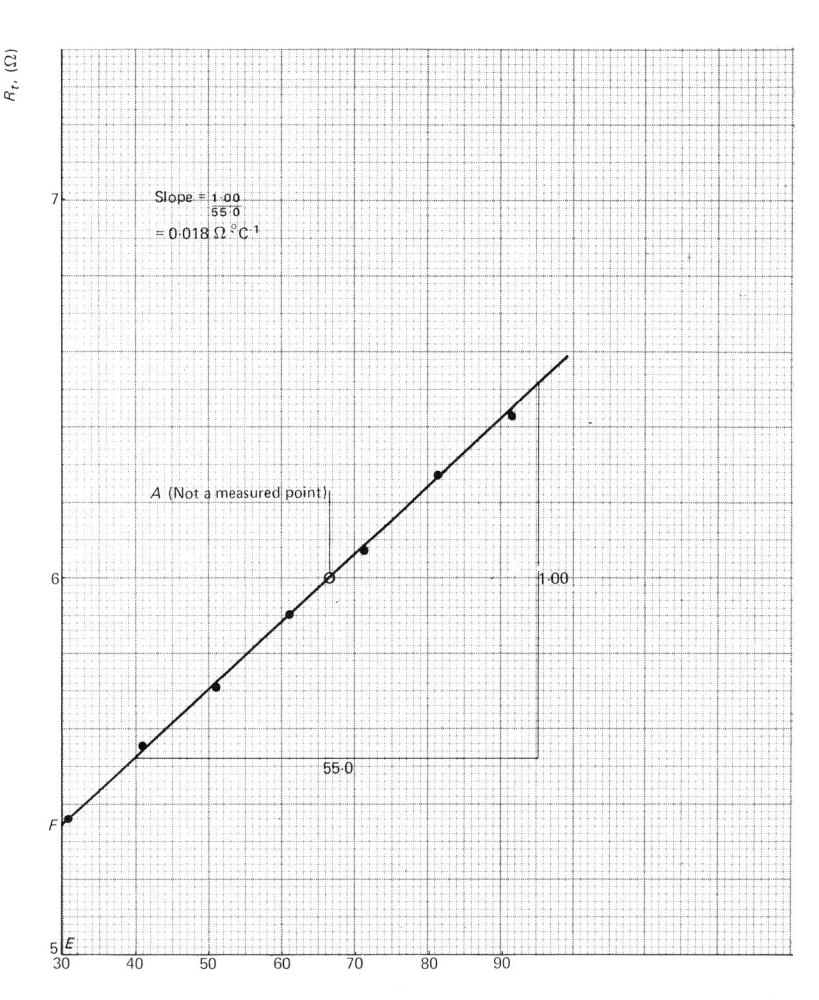

point on the line (this does not have to be a measured point). Since this point lies on the line it can be substituted into the equation,

$$y = mx + c$$

giving,

$$\bar{y} = m\bar{x} + c$$

from which c can be found. We can also find the intercept on the x axis which is given by $-c/m$.

Returning to our specific problem. The slope m of the graph has been calculated as $0.018 \ \Omega \ °C^{-1}$. We now choose any point A on the line, and read off its coordinates,

$$\bar{y} = R_t = 6.0 \ \Omega, \ \bar{x} = t = 66.3°C$$

and using

$$\bar{y} = m\bar{x} + c$$

we obtain

$$6.0 = 0.018 \times 66.3 + c$$

17

∴ $c = 4{\cdot}81\ \Omega$ which is R_0 the resistance at 0°C.

Compare this with the value of 4·8 obtained by direct measurement from the graph in Fig. 1.6. The value of 4·81 is the more accurate since a better straight line has been judged in Fig. 1.9, the point A has been chosen to be exactly on the line and no large extrapolation has been necessary.

Log-log graphs

We have seen that by using a suitable choice of variables a straight line graph can be obtained if the dependence of one variable on the other is known. In the case of the parabolic water jet we know that,

$$y = \left(\frac{g}{2v^2}\right)x^2$$

and we can plot y against x^2 to obtain a straight line graph.

However situations do arise where the exact form of the dependence between variables is not known. If we consider the example of a heated filament, where all the energy evolved is lost as radiation, the relationship between the potential difference V across the filament, and the current I through it is given by,

$$V \propto I^n$$

where n is the power term and is not equal to unity because the temperature of the filament, and hence its resistance, depend on the current I in some way.

The equation is now written in the form,

$$V = DI^n$$

where D is a constant.

To obtain a straight line graph from a series of results for V and I the equation has to be in the form of $y = mx + c$. This can be done by taking logs to the base ten of the equation,

$$\log_{10} V = \log_{10} DI^n$$

This gives,

$$\log_{10} V = \log_{10} D + \log_{10} I^n$$

$$\log_{10} V = n \log_{10} I + \log_{10} D$$

Comparing this with the equation for a straight line $y = mx + c$ we see that y is given by $\log_{10} V$, x is given by $\log_{10} I$, the slope m is given by n, and the intercept c on the y axis is given by $\log_{10} D$.

Plotting $\log_{10} V$ against $\log_{10} I$ we obtain the straight line graph shown in Fig. 1.10. In practice D is less than unity so that $\log_{10} D$ is negative as shown in the figure.

Plotting a log graph can be rather difficult when bar numbers are encountered for the first time. Sometimes bar numbers can be avoided by converting the units used into smaller ones. For example instead of plotting $\log_{10} (0{\cdot}5\ \text{m}) = \bar{1}{\cdot}6990$ we could use $\log_{10} (500\ \text{mm}) = 2{\cdot}6990$ and if necessary convert back in a later calculation to the initial units.

Sometimes bar numbers are unavoidable but a great deal of effort

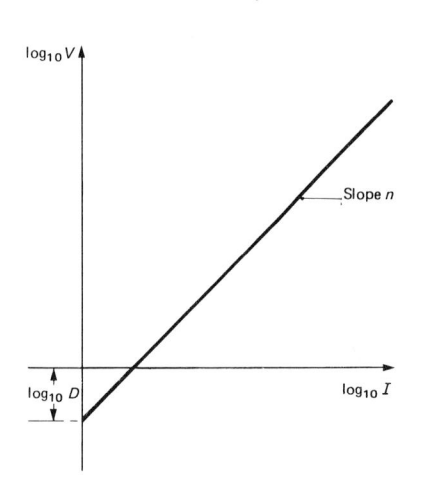

Fig. 1.10 $\log_{10} V$ against $\log_{10} I$.

Fig. 1.11 Plotting point (1·3421, 2·6934).

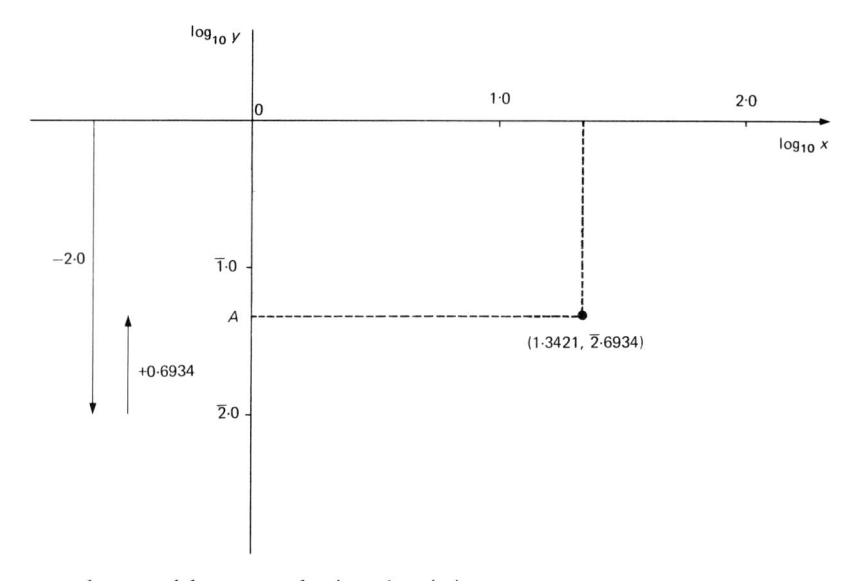

can be saved by remembering that it is not necessary to convert them into wholly negative numbers in order to plot them. What you have to remember is that $\bar{1}\cdot6934$ means $-1+0\cdot6934$ and there is no need to convert this to $-0\cdot3066$. Consider how a point having coordinates $(1\cdot3421, \bar{2}\cdot6934)$ can be plotted (see Fig. 1.11).

The value 1·3421 on the $\log_{10} x$ axis can be easily located and for

Fig. 1.12 Labelling axes for a log plot.

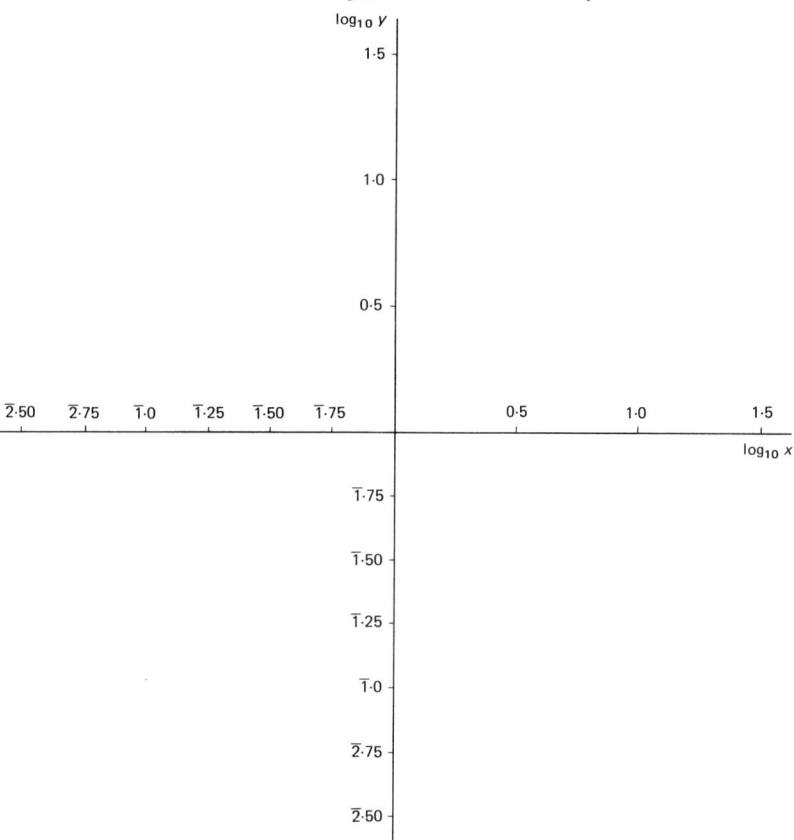

19

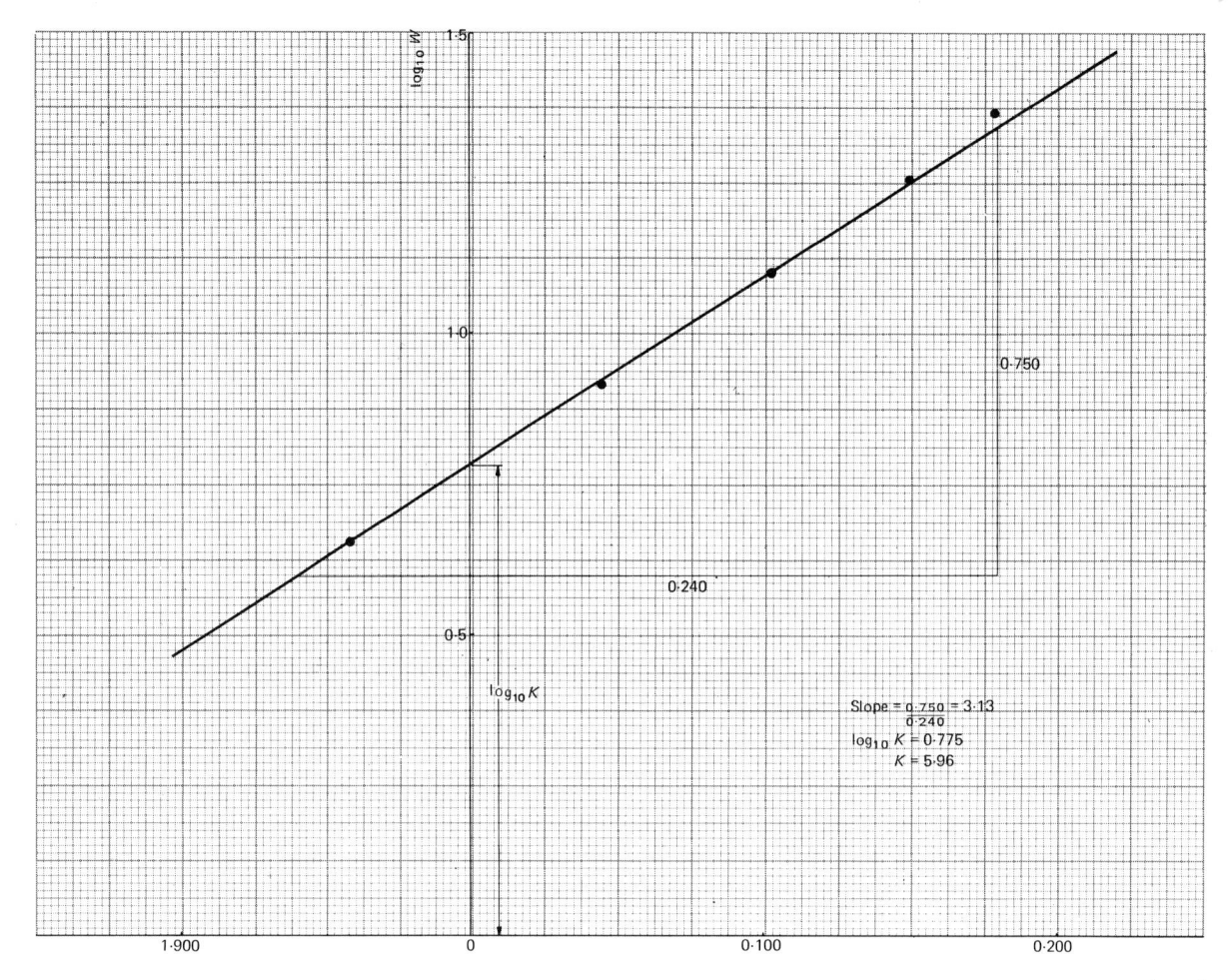

Fig. 1.13 Graph of $\log_{10} W$ against $\log_{10} R$.

the $\bar{2}\cdot6934$ value we consider this as $-2+0\cdot6934$. We go down the $\log_{10} y$ axis to $\bar{2}\cdot0$ in a negative direction (that is $-2\cdot0$) and then go up $0\cdot6934$ in the positive direction and arrive at point A which has the value $\bar{2}\cdot6934$ and hence the point can be plotted. A similar procedure can be adopted when plotting bar quantities along the $\log_{10} x$ axis. Thus when plotting a log graph where bar numbers are involved the axes should be labelled as shown in Fig. 1.12. When the scales are written in this way there is ease of plotting the results and measured negative intercepts can be quickly and easily anti-logged.

A complete log graph is shown in Fig. 1.13. This graph is concerned with the power dissipated in a heated filament of resistance R. Theory shows that the power W is given by,

$$W = KR^4$$

where K is a constant and R is the resistance. The results for such an experiment are shown in Table 1.3.

If $\log_{10} W$ is plotted against $\log_{10} R$ as shown in the figure $\log_{10} K$ will be obtained as the intercept on the $\log_{10} W$ axis and the slope should have a value of 4.

Power W, (watts)	Resistance R, (ohms)
4·41	0·91
8·11	1·11
12·59	1·27
17·70	1·41
23·88	1·51
$\log_{10} W$	$\log_{10} R$
0·644	$\bar{1}$·959
0·909	0·045
1·100	0·104
1·248	0·149
1·378	0·179

Table 1.3.

It can be seen from the graph that the intercept on the $\log_{10} W$ axis is 0.775 so that $\log_{10} K = 0.775$ and hence K has a numerical value of 5.96. The value of the slope is found to be 3.13 rather than the value of 4. This is an interesting result which indicates that one of the basic assumptions used in the theory to derive the equation $W = KR^4$ is incorrect. The incorrect assumption was that all the heat is lost from the filament by radiation. In fact some of the heat will be lost by conduction through the leads.

Similar procedures to those already described can be followed when Naperian logarithms are used. As a reminder if $\log_e 0.4$ is required we can obtain it in the following way,

$$\log_e 0.4 = \log_e 4 \times 10^{-1} = \log_e 4 + \log_e 10^{-1}$$
$$= 1.386 + \bar{3}.6974 = \bar{1}.0834$$

However it is usually easier to convert $\log_e$ to $\log_{10}$ for plotting purposes using,

$$\log_e x = \log_e 10 \times \log_{10} x = 2.3026 \log_{10} x$$

Log-linear graphs

To illustrate this type of graph we consider a radioactive decay process which is described by,

$$N = N_0 e^{-\lambda t}$$

where N_0 is the number of atoms present at an arbitrary zero time, N is the number remaining after the lapse of a further time interval t and λ is the decay constant. Taking logs to the base e we obtain,

$$\log_e N = \log_e N_0 - \lambda t$$
$$2.303 \log_{10} N = 2.303 \log_{10} N_0 - \lambda t$$
$$\log_{10} N = \log_{10} N_0 - \lambda t / 2.303$$
$$\log_{10} N = \log_{10} N_0 - 0.4343 \lambda t$$

The rate at which particles are decaying in a radioactive material in a small time interval can be measured with suitable counting equipment. If this rate, measured after a time t is represented by R then,

$$R = R_0 e^{-\lambda t}$$
$$\log_{10} R = \log_{10} R_0 - 0.4343 \lambda t$$
$$\log_{10} R = -0.4343 \lambda t + \log_{10} R_0$$

where R_0 is the decay rate at the arbitrary zero of time. This equation is similar to that for $\log_{10} N$ above.

The final equation above for $\log_{10} R$ is in the form $y = mx + c$ and if $\log_{10} R$ is plotted as ordinate and t as abscissa we obtain a straight line graph having a slope of -0.4343λ and an intercept of $\log_{10} R_0$ on the $\log_{10} R$ axis.

The type of graph expected for the $\log_{10} R$ against t plot is shown in Fig. 1.14. The theory implies a negative slope and this is shown in the figure.

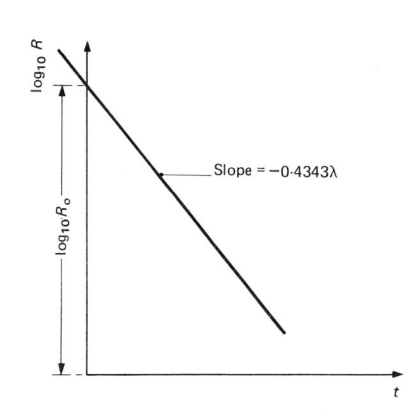

Fig. 1.14 $\log_{10} R$ against Time (t).

In a log-linear plot bar numbers can be dealt with in the same way as in a log-log plot.

It is possible to avoid the labour of looking up the logs and plotting them on linear graph paper by using log-log or log-linear paper, speci-

Fig. 1.15 Log-log paper.

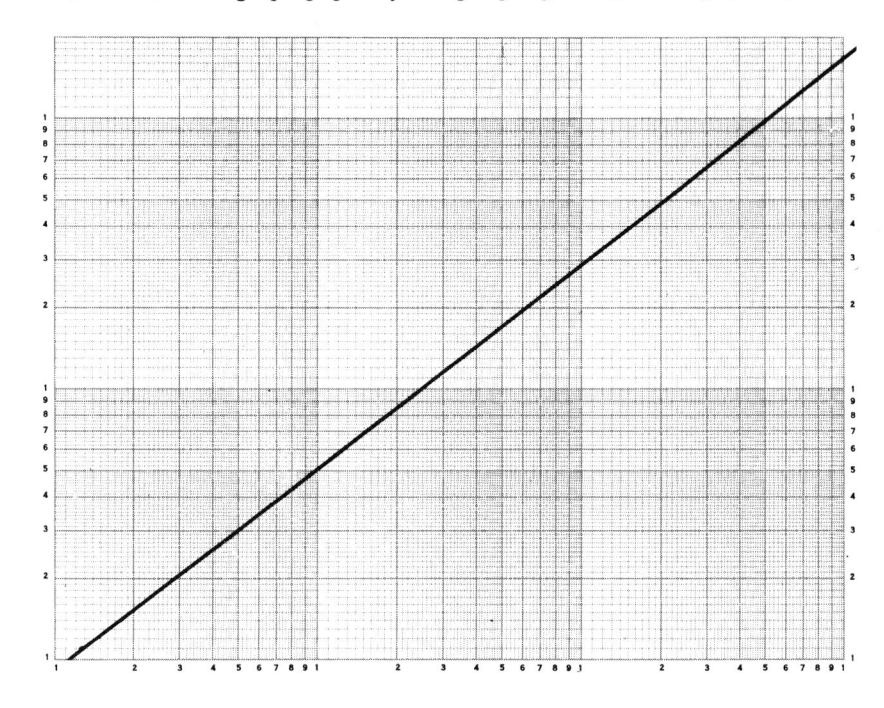

Fig. 1.16 Log–linear paper.

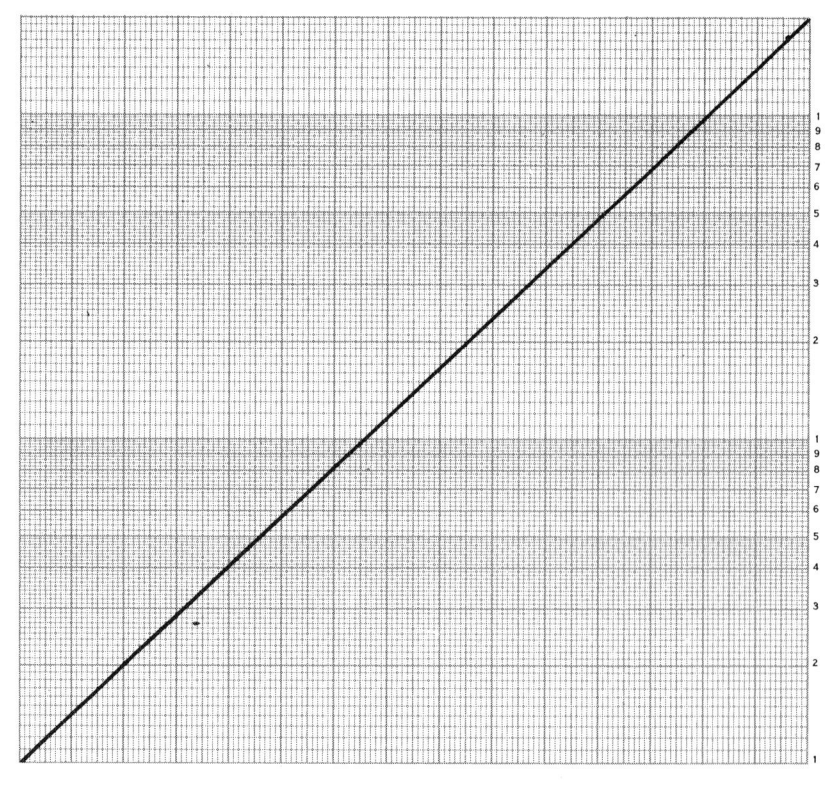

mens of which are shown in Fig. 1.15 and Fig. 1.16. On such paper the spacing of the lines follows a $\log_{10}$ scale so that if variables x or y are plotted on such a scale the same distribution is obtained as if the $\log_{10}$ had been plotted on linear paper.

Fig. 1.17 Power (W) against Resistance (R) plotted on log–log paper.

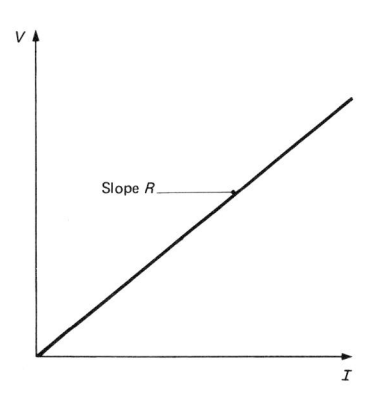

Fig. 1.18.

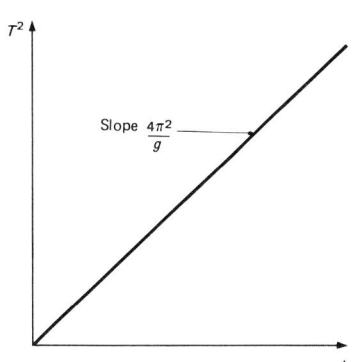

Fig. 1.19.

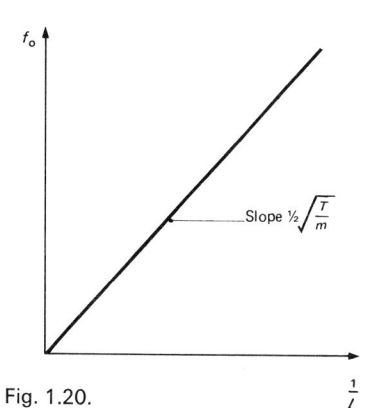

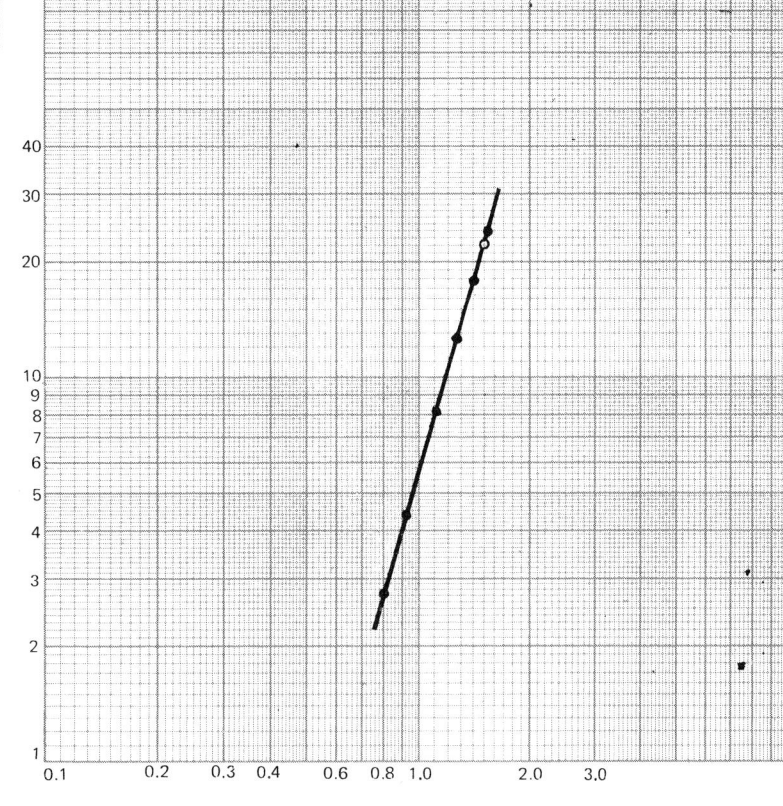

Fig. 1.20.

As an example of the use of such paper the results used for the graph in Fig. 1.13 are replotted as shown in Fig. 1.17.

The straightness of the line shows that the equation plotted has the form $W = KR^n$ but it is not possible to obtain n from it in the usual simple way. If n is required the following procedure must be used. The equation is first written in the $\log_{10}$ form,

$$\log_{10} W = n \log_{10} R + \log_{10} K$$

and then two points are chosen on the line, for example $W = 22$, $R = 1 \cdot 5$ and $W = 2 \cdot 7$, $R = 0 \cdot 8$. These are substituted in the log equation,

$$\log_{10} 22 = n \log_{10} 1 \cdot 5 + \log_{10} K$$

$$\log_{10} 2 \cdot 7 = n \log_{10} 0 \cdot 8 + \log_{10} K$$

These two equations are subtracted giving,

$$\log_{10} 22 - \log_{10} 2 \cdot 7 = n(\log_{10} 1 \cdot 5 - \log_{10} 0 \cdot 8)$$

$$\therefore n = \frac{\log_{10} 22 - \log_{10} 2\cdot 7}{\log_{10} 1\cdot 5 - \log_{10} 0\cdot 8} = \frac{\log_{10} 22/2\cdot 7}{\log_{10} 1\cdot 5/0\cdot 8}$$

$$= \frac{\log_{10} 8\cdot 16}{\log_{10} 1\cdot 88} = 3\cdot 3$$

As a general rule where accuracy is required it is better to plot a log graph on linear paper, since it is difficult to judge the intervals

Form	Example	Graph
$y = mx$. Plot y against x and obtain slope m.	$V = IR$ (Ohm's law). Plot V as ordinate y, I as abscissa x. Obtain slope R. See Fig. 1.18.	
	$T = 2\pi\sqrt{\dfrac{l}{g}}$ (Period of simple pendulum). Convert to $T^2 = 4\pi^2\dfrac{l}{g}$. Plot T^2 as ordinate y, l as abscissa x. Obtain slope $4\pi^2/g$. See Fig. 1.19.	
	$f_0 = \dfrac{1}{2l}\sqrt{\dfrac{T}{m}}$ (Fundamental frequency of a sonometer wire). Plot f_0 as ordinate y, $1/l$ as abscissa x. Obtain slope $\dfrac{1}{2}\sqrt{\dfrac{T}{m}}$. See Fig. 1.20.	
$y = mx + c$. Plot y against x and obtain slope m. Intercept on y axis is c. Intercept on x axis is $-c/m$.	$R_t = R_0(1 + \alpha t)$ (Variation of resistance with temperature). Convert to $R_t = (R_0\alpha)t + R_0$. Plot R_t as ordinate y, t as abscissa x. Obtain slope $R_0\alpha$. Intercept on R_t axis is R_0. Intercept on t axis is $-1/\alpha$. See Fig. 1.21.	
	$T = 2\pi\sqrt{\dfrac{k^2 + h^2}{gh}}$ (Period of compound pendulum). Convert to $T^2 = 4\pi^2(k/gh + h/g)$ and then to $hT^2 = 4\pi^2 k^2/g + 4\pi^2 h^2/g$. Plot hT^2 as ordinate y, h^2 as abscissa x. Obtain slope $4\pi^2/g$. Intercept on hT^2 axis is $4\pi^2 k^2/g$. Intercept on h^2 axis is $-k^2$. See Fig. 1.22.	
$y = Dx^n$. where D is a constant and n is an unknown power. Use $\log y = n \log x + \log D$. Plot $\log y$ against $\log x$ and obtain slope n. Intercept on $\log y$ axis is $\log D$. Intercept on $\log x$ axis is $-\log D/n$.	$V = DI^n$ (Relationship between voltage and current in a heated filament). Convert to $\log V = n \log I + \log D$. Plot $\log V$ as ordinate y, $\log I$ as abscissa x. Obtain slope n. Intercept on $\log V$ axis is $\log D$. Intercept on $\log I$ axis is $-\dfrac{\log D}{n}$. See Fig. 1.23.	

between the lines on the log paper. If however speed is required for the confirmation of the form of the equation $y = kx^n$ then log-log paper is satisfactory.

In your work you will not use log-log graphs very often since the form of the dependence of the variables in your experiments is usually obvious but the log-log plot is a powerful tool in advanced experimental physics. Frequently the first thing which is done with a set of results is to make a log-log plot of them so that the power n can be obtained for various ranges of the results.

Summary

To summarise the whole of this section on graphs we can say that we almost always aim to produce a straight line graph and that this is done by the correct choice of variables.

Area under a curve

Quite frequently the product of two variable quantities has a definite physical meaning. For example if v is the velocity and t is the time we know that the product $v \times t$ represents the distance travelled. Similarly we know that if F is a force and S is the distance moved by the point of application of the force then the product $F \times S$ represents the work done.

We have to ask the question, if y is plotted against x how can the product xy be obtained from the graph? This is fairly easy to understand if we consider the examples quoted above. If results of v and t had been plotted graphically, then the area of a square of the graph paper represents, to scale, a definite number of units of the product $v \times t$. If a unit on one axis represents a velocity of 4 ms^{-1} and a unit on the other axis a time of $5\ s$ then the area of one square represents $4 \times 5 = 20\ m$ distance covered. Similarly if F is plotted against S and one unit represents $20\ N$ on the force axis, and one unit represents $5\ m$ on the distance axis, the area of one square represents $20 \times 5 = 100$ J of work done.

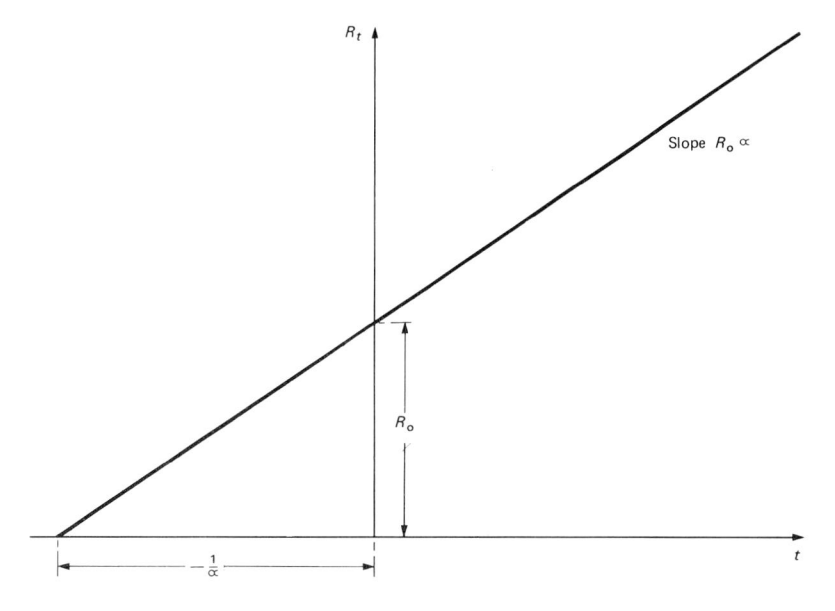

Fig. 1.21.

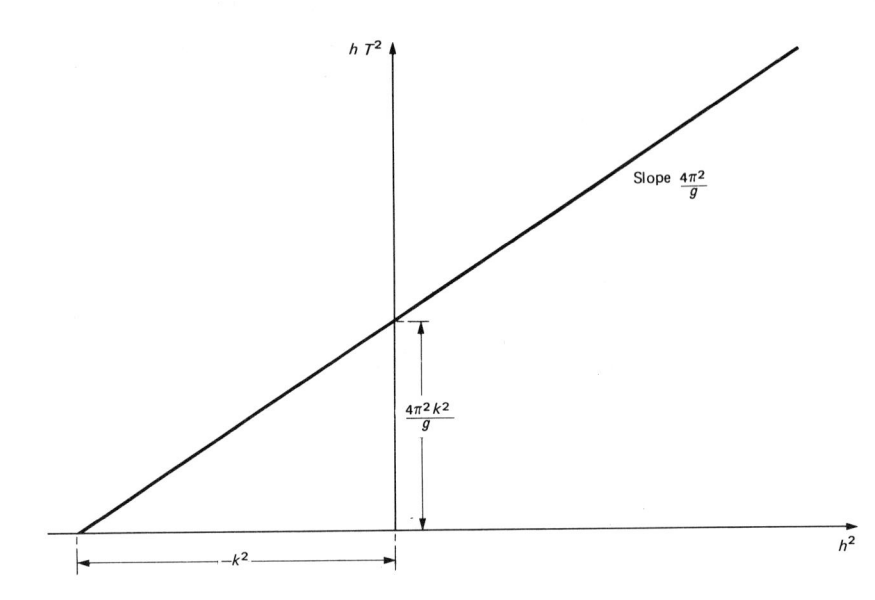

Fig. 1.22.

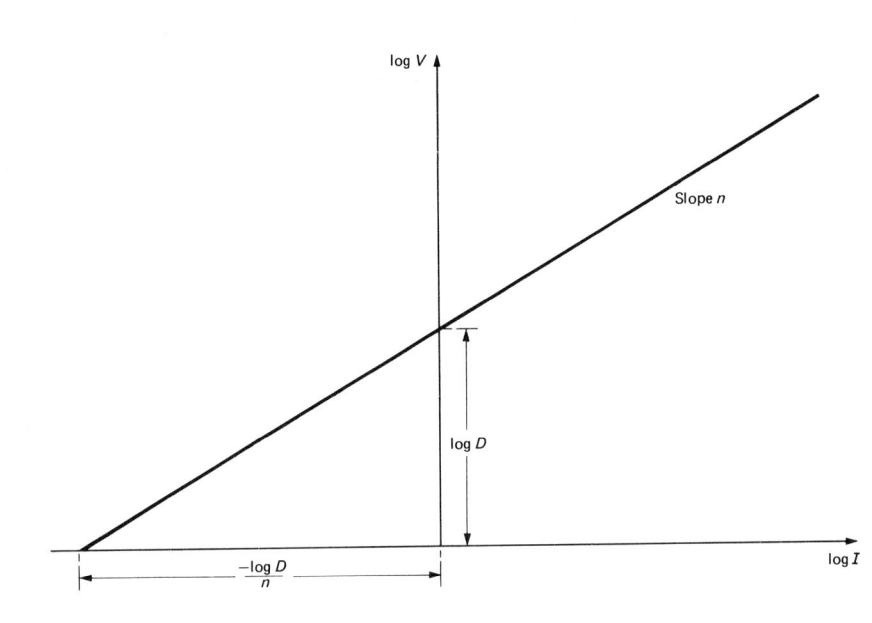

Fig. 1.23.

Figure 1.24 shows a constant force of 60 N moving its point of application and has been drawn using the scale previously quoted. The area $OABC$, which contains twelve unit squares, represents 1200 J, which is the work done by the 60 N force when moving its point of application through a distance of 20 m.

Even if the force is not a constant we find the same rule still applies. The graph drawn in Fig. 1.25 represents a force which is changing in magnitude as it moves its point of application. Suppose the force increases in a very small distance BD from a value represented by AB to a value represented by CD. Since the work done equals the average

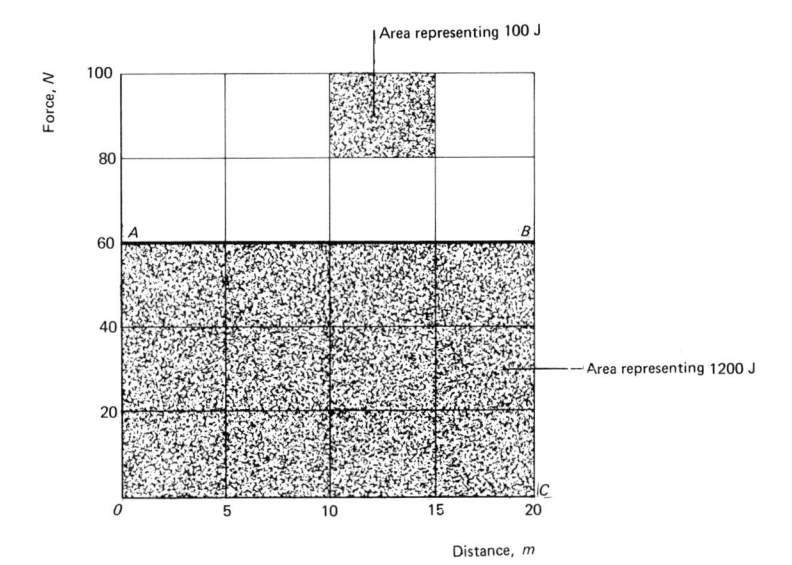

Fig. 1.24 Constant force moving its point of application.

force times the distance the work done is represented by the shaded area $ABDC$. By considering every small distance interval between O and Q in the same way it follows that the total work done by the varying force in moving its point of application a distance OQ is given by the area OPQ which is the area between the force–distance curve and the distance axis. In the figure the area OPQ is about 28 squares, representing 2800 J of work. The area $GPQH$, about 17·5 squares, represents the work done in the distance between H and Q and is 1750 J.

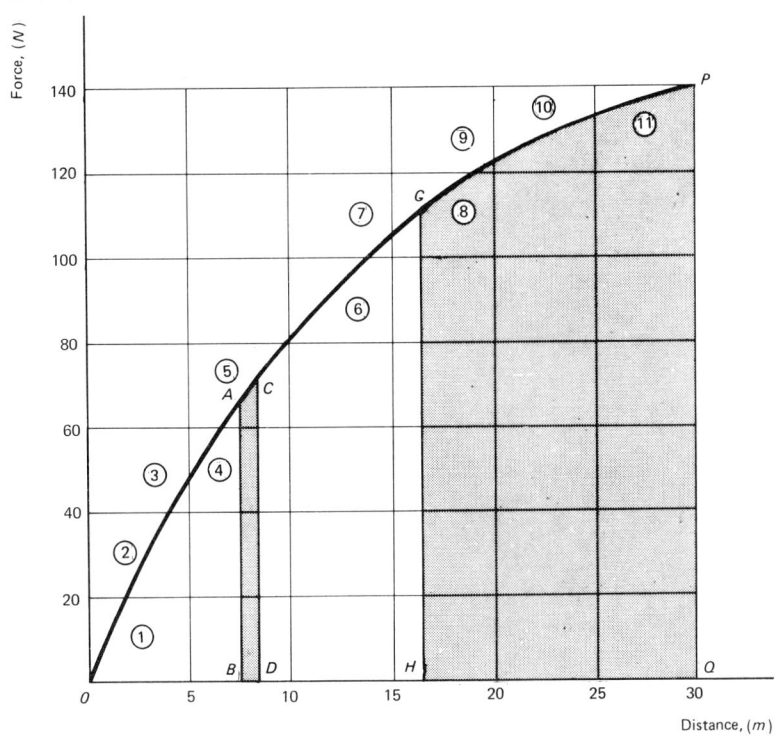

Fig. 1.25 Variable force moving its point of application.

27

When calculating areas from graphs two important precautions must be observed:
(1) a true origin (0, 0) must be used and must be shown on the graph
(2) the area measured must be that between the curve and the correct axis

Unless calculus is used it is difficult to give a hard and fast rule about the second precaution, but a moment's thought should enable the correct axis to be chosen. In the example of the force against distance graph an increase in the force without any increase in distance means the performance of no work; this increase in force would be represented by a vertical line on the graph and there is zero area between this line and the distance axis representing zero work as is required. Hence we require the area between the curve and the distance axis to find the total work done. Those of you who are familiar with calculus should have no difficulty in deciding upon the correct area to measure.

The simplest way to assess the area enclosed by the graph is to count the squares under it. First add up all the whole squares enclosed. Then examine all squares through which the line (straight line or curve) passes. If more than half of the square is under the curve count it as a whole square, if less than half ignore it. Provided the squares are small compared with the total area enclosed a reasonably accurate total count can be made in this way. Applying this idea to Fig. 1.25 we can see that *OPQ* encloses 23 whole squares and in addition to these,

square number   1 counts as 1
square number   2 counts as 0
square number   3 counts as 0
square number   4 counts as 1
square number   5 counts as 0
square number   6 counts as 1
square number   7 counts as 0
square number   8 counts as 1
square number   9 counts as 0
square number 10 counts as 0
square number 11 counts as 1
                    Total   5

The total area under the graph is thus 28 units approximately. Fig. 1.25 is not really a good example to use as the squares are rather too large (each is approximately 4% of the area under the curve) but if a graph is drawn on mm graph paper and the 1 mm^2 squares are used for counting good results can be obtained.

Chapter 2 Hints on Plotting Graphs

We always aim to spread the available results as widely as possible over the graph page so that we can draw an accurate line through them. This involves choosing the scales appropriately. Simple scale divisions should always be used so that each small square is either 1, 2 or 5 times a power of 10. For example 0·1, 0·2, 0·5; 10, 20, 50; and so on. Never choose a scale based on one small square being 3 or 4 times a power of 10, as it is very difficult to plot points accurately on such a scale. If you examine the horizontal scale of the student's graph in Test 1 and try to see how the points were placed in their horizontal positions the difficulty will become obvious.

When a restricted range of results is used which does not approach the origin it is best to set up false origins so that the points can be made to cover the whole graph page. This gives a more accurate slope but means that the true intercepts have to be calculated rather than measured from the graph. An example of the choice of a false origin and the consequent increase of scale which can be made has already been shown on pages 16 and 17. When you try Tests 1 and 5 you will find that the range of results is wide enough to make false origins unnecessary but such origins will be useful in Tests 2 and 3. Test 4 involves measuring intercepts using a curve rather than a straight line and although such intercepts could be calculated it is far easier to use true origins and measure them from the graph. The sketch graph in Test 4 shows this (see Fig. 4.4(b)).

The points themselves are best plotted as either ringed dots ⊙ or crosses ×; this avoids confusion with odd marks on the graph paper. The axes should be drawn in ink or ballpoint and labelled with the name and units of the quantity involved. The graph should be given a title and if there is a suitable blank area on it this may be used to draw up the table of results. A soft sharp pencil should be used to draw the graph line as this may have to be rubbed out several times, particularly when drawing curves rather than straight lines. When drawing a curve (or a straight line) through experimental points do not join up the individual points by straight lines as shown by the dotted lines in Fig. 2.1 but put a smooth curve (or a best straight line) through them. Such a line is very probably the true variation of y with x. Real phenomena almost never show irregular variations like the dotted line. Such variations are almost always due to instrument and observer error. This can be shown by repeating the set of observations which are shown as crosses in Fig. 2.2. Slight variations will be obtained in the results but the same smooth curve is obtained as before.

You will meet a few examples of 'dot to dot' plotting. One of these

Fig. 2.1 Drawing a curve through experimental points.

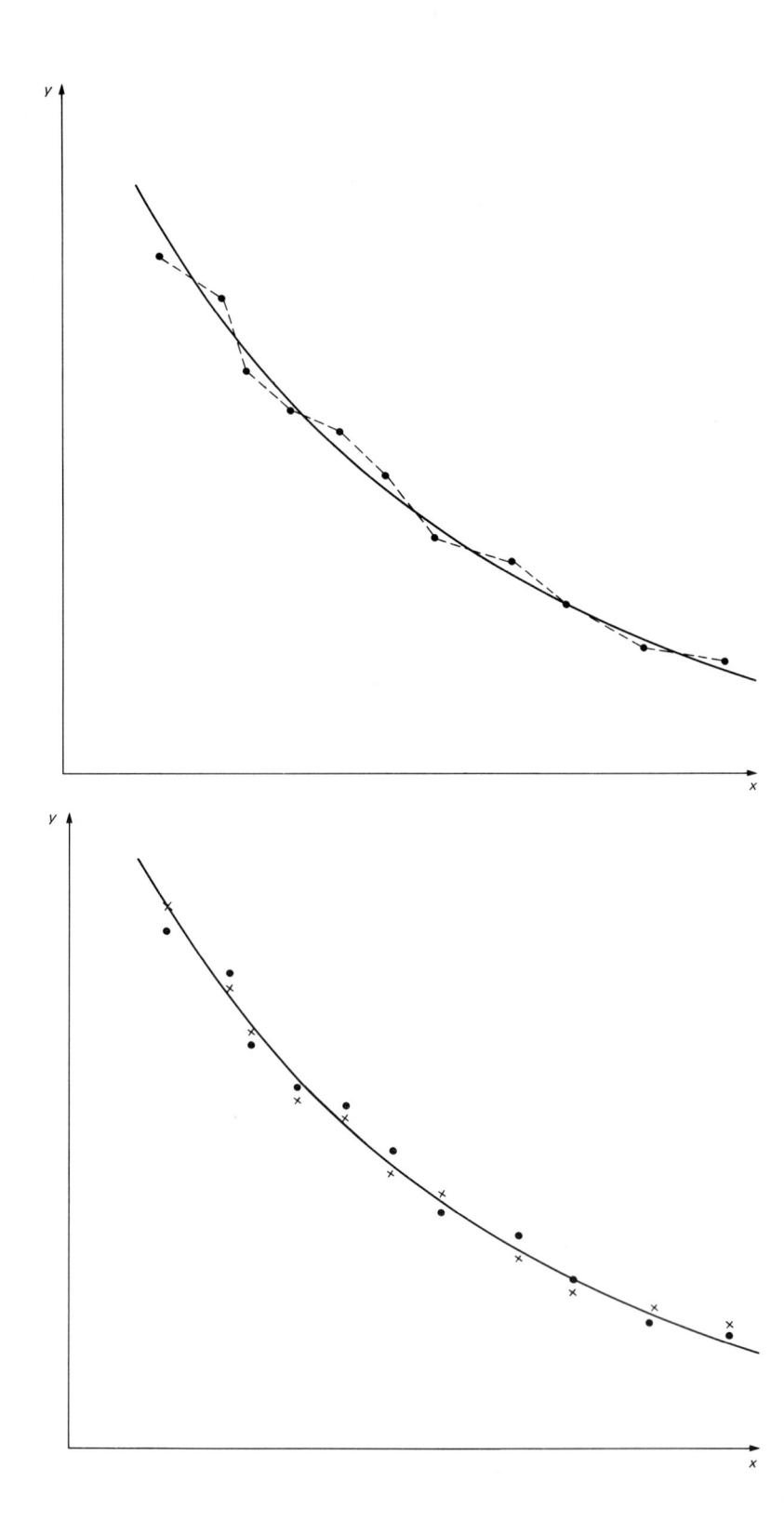

Fig. 2.2 Repeat results plotted.

Fig. 2.3 Correction chart for meter reading.

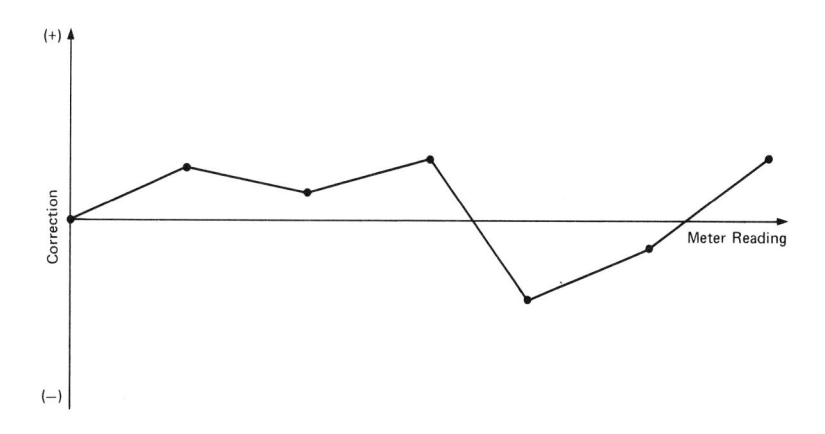

is the calibration of an ammeter or voltmeter by use of a potentiometer in which a correction chart for the meter reading is made up. See Fig. 2.3. There is no obvious trend in such a chart and the correction we use depends on the actual meter reading involved. Correction between measured points has to be done by interpolation. Another example is the plotting of random processes. The background counting experiment (Test 12) shows this. You are asked to plot the number of counts of background radiation registered by a geiger counter in sequential one minute intervals (see Fig. 2.4). Each one minute count has no bearing on the previous one or the following one and a smooth curve cannot be drawn. If the vertical scale was made small enough it might be possible to draw a best straight line parallel to the time axis which would give the average counts per minute but a different form of graph is really required to do this accurately. This will become clear when you do the test.

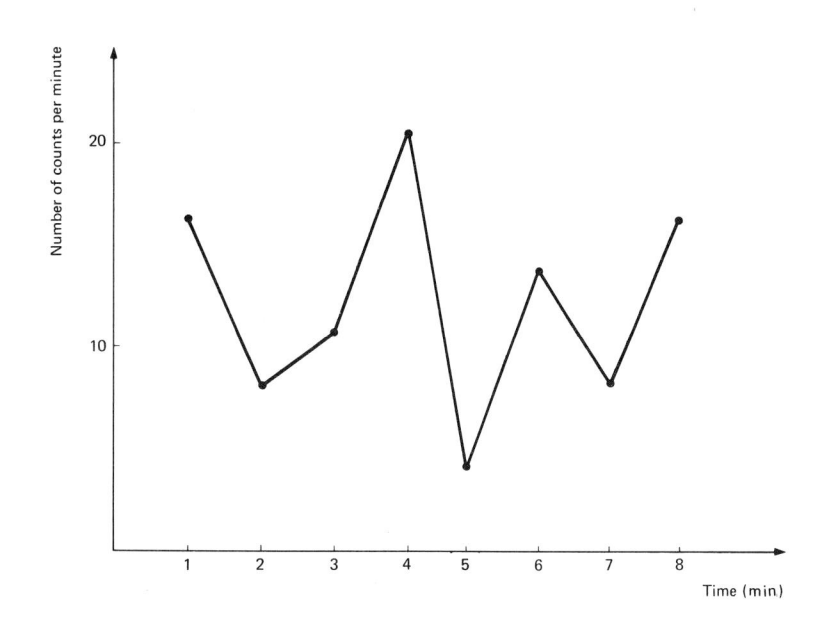

Fig. 2.4 Background counting experiment results.

Fig. 2.5 Best straight line.

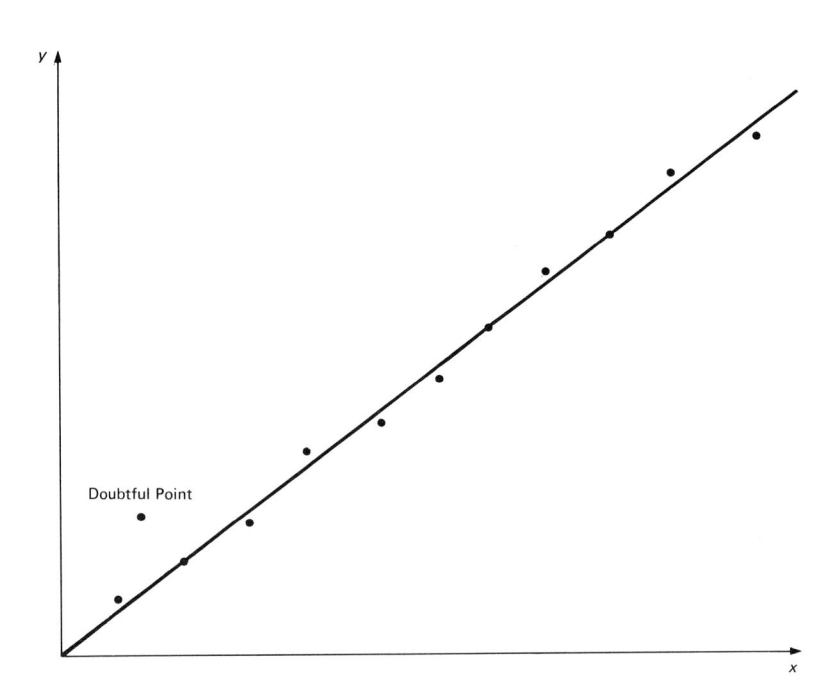

Doubtful Point

When drawing a straight line you have to position your ruler (clear plastic is best) so that as many points as possible lie on the line. Those which do not should be roughly equally distributed on both sides of the line. Ignore 'doubtful' points when drawing the line but recheck the readings leading to them (see Fig. 2.5).

Before drawing the line you should decide from your knowledge of the theory whether it should pass through the origin, (assuming you are using a true origin) that is, whether you are plotting $y = mx$ or $y = mx + c$. If it should be $y = mx$ and your line does not pass through the origin then either it is not the best straight line or there is a systematic error in x or y so that an intercept is formed as explained on page 14.

Another way of drawing a best straight line is to divide the points into two equal sections. Find and plot the average values of the co-ordinates for each section $(\bar{y}_1, \bar{x}_1)$ and $(\bar{y}_2, \bar{x}_2)$. Join these two points as shown in Fig. 2.6 to give the best straight line. 'Doubtful' points must not be used in calculating $(\bar{y}_1, \bar{x}_1)$ and $(\bar{y}_2, \bar{x}_2)$. Once you have developed an 'eye' for the best straight line you will find that the first method described is quite accurate and very much quicker than the second method, but do remember the considerations about scatter and 'doubtful' points mentioned on page 11.

When drawing a curve 'freehand' always have your hand on the concave side of the curve. Curves are much easier to draw using a flexible rubber strip although these cannot be bent into very small radius bends. Similar considerations to the straight line case hold when setting your rubber strip to draw the best curve.

An experimental curve may show a maximum or a minimum. An example of this is the curve in Test 4 whose minimum is used in several

Fig. 2.6 Best straight line.

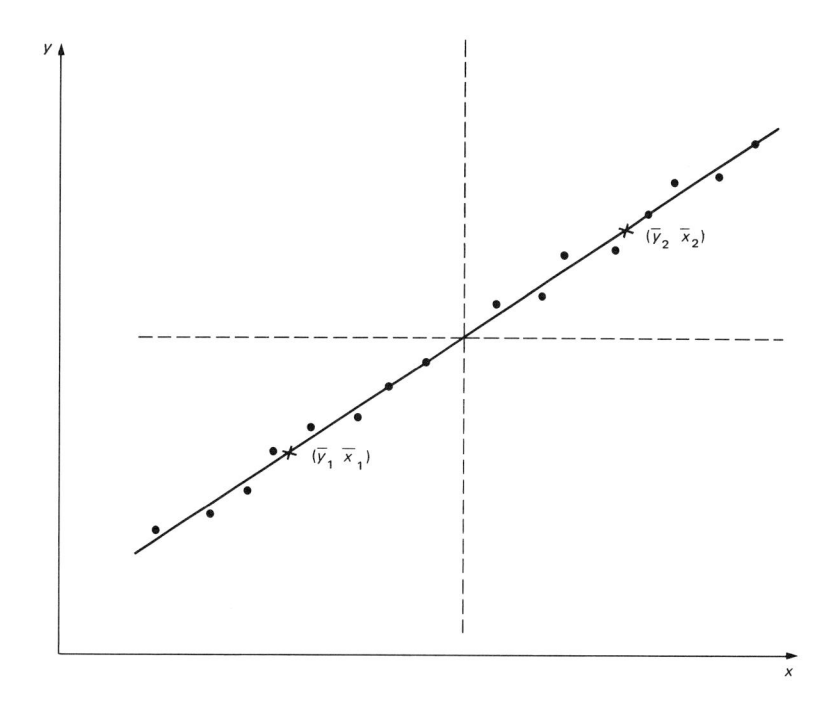

ways, (see Fig. A.4). Near the minimum some extra experimental results have been taken so that the minimum can be drawn accurately. This is an example of a fairly obvious general rule that it is wise to take extra readings wherever a rapid change of slope of the graph occurs. In the example above however a few more readings say at $u = 23$, 24 cm and at $u > 70$ cm would be helpful. Another situation

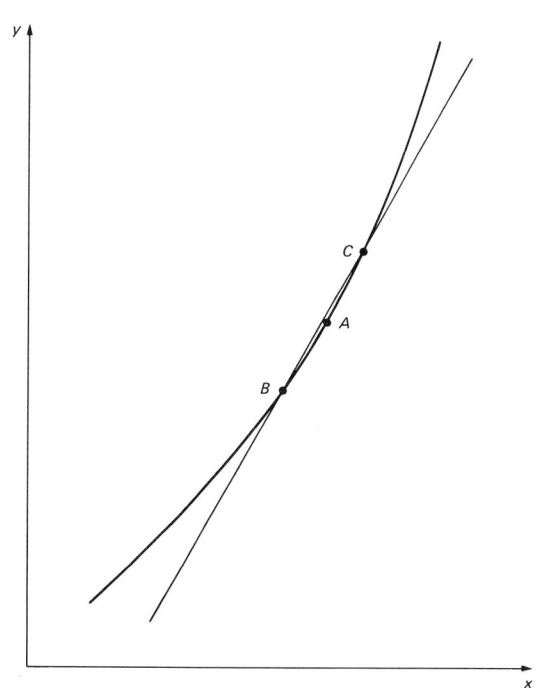

Fig. 2.7 Drawing of tangent to a curve.

Tangent to a curve

where extra readings are useful is when an intercept is to be measured using true origins. Extra points near the axis on which the intercept is measured will improve its accuracy by enabling a better straight line to be judged.

Very often when dealing with curves the tangent (slope) of the curve is required. This is not at all easy to judge particularly when the curve is a shallow one but there are two methods which are fairly quick and reasonably accurate.

Suppose in Fig. 2.7 the slope at point *A* is required. The curve is fairly shallow so that the tangent cannot be easily judged. However the slope at *A* can be obtained by marking two points *B* and *C* at equal small distances along the curve on either side of *A* and drawing a straight line through them. Provided *B* and *C* are close to *A* and the curvature is fairly constant in this region the line *BC* will have the same slope as a true tangent to the curve at *A*.

If the curvature of the graph is changing rapidly near *A* the points *B* and *C* will have to be very close to *A* or line *BC* will not be parallel to a tangent through *A*.

You might like to try an exercise along these lines. Take the results given in Test 1 and plot *h* against *t* choosing sensible scales. Draw the curve and mark on it the point $h = 0.44$, $t = 0.3$. This is point *A*.

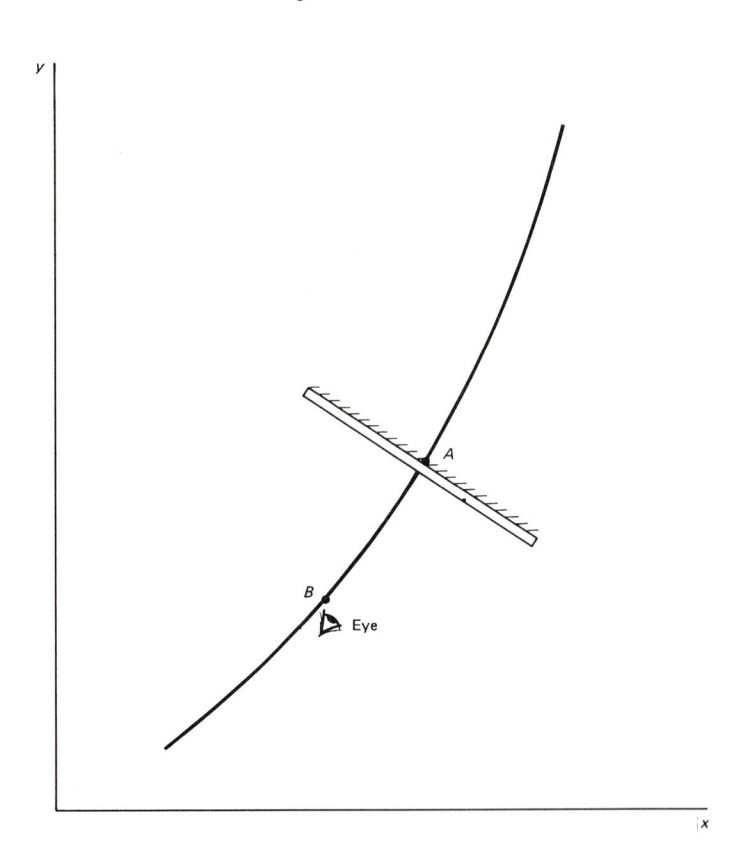

Fig. 2.8 Mirror method for drawing a tangent to a curve.

Draw the best tangent you can through *A*. Now mark in *B* and *C* close to *A*, say 5 mm on either side, and draw the line *BC*. Repeat for other positions of *B* and *C*. You should observe that as the distance *BC* gets larger the slope of the line *BC* gets less and is a progressively worse approximation to the tangent through *A*.

Another method which is just as quick though less accurate is to use a plane mirror on the graph page to find the normal to the curve. Place a plane mirror (3 inches × 1 inch is a convenient size) on the graph as shown in Fig. 2.8 with its silvered surface coincident with *A*. View the section *AB* of the graph at the same time as its virtual image in the mirror and adjust the mirror until the line *AB* appears to join its image to form a smooth curve. That is, there must be no kink at the mirror silvered surface. The judgement of this requires practice and if in doubt you should ask for a demonstration from your teacher. The mirror is now normal to the curve at *A* and you can draw the normal by running a pencil along the back of the mirror. Remove the mirror and draw a perpendicular to the normal at *A*. This is the tangent to the curve at *A*.

In general the first method is the more accurate but the second has the advantage of placing the tangent at *A* rather than slightly to one side at *BC*.

Chapter 3   The Assessment of Experimental Errors

Up to this stage you may never have questioned your ability to make accurate measurements in the laboratory and will probably have trusted your instruments' readings implicitly. A little thought will show however that there is always an inherent uncertainty when a physical measurement is made. This may be due to the ability (or lack of it) of the observer or the limited accuracy of the instrument used. A few examples will make this clear.

Observer (random) error

On page 9 the motion of a water jet from a horizontal pipe is described. By measuring the parabolic path of the jet, the acceleration due to gravity g can be deduced using the equation,

$$y = \left(\frac{g}{2v^2}\right)x^2$$

where v is the velocity at which the water emerges from the jet. This velocity can be found simply by collecting the water in a measuring cylinder over a known time measured with a stop watch.

$$\text{Velocity } v = \frac{\text{volume collected per second}}{\text{cross sectional area of jet}}$$

If the water is supplied from a constant head device we can assume that v is almost certainly constant but if successive one minute collections are made we will find the volumes collected are different. We might find them to be 50·5, 51·0, 50·0, 49·5 and 51·0 cm³. This gives a mean value of 50·4 cm³. The deviations of the individual values from this mean value are too large to be accounted for by the accuracy with which the measuring cylinder is read. (This is calibrated in units of 1 cm³ and can be read to an accuracy of $\pm 0·5$ cm³).

The deviations are due to random factors such as the speed with which the cylinder was removed from under the water jet, the experimenter's personal reaction time in using the stop watch, odd drips of water in the cylinder and so on. The more readings that are taken the closer the average value will come to the true one and the more reliance can be placed on the result. To prove this and to calculate the size of the probable error in such a result we have to use some statistical theory which is rather beyond the scope of this book. We can however conclude that repeated measurements of the same quantity are bound to lead to errors, the size of which is minimised by taking the average of a large number of readings.

Instrument error

The other source of error involved in measuring something is the inherent inaccuracy of the instrument used. As a general rough rule

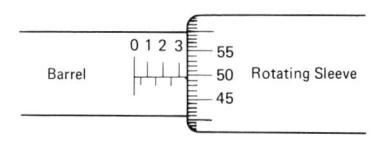

Fig. 3.1 Micrometer screw gauge reading 3·500 ± 0·005 mm.

you cannot trust an instrument to accurately measure a quantity which is smaller than the smallest calibration unit on its scale. For example if you measured a current of 2·5 mA on a meter with a range 0–25 mA calibrated in 1 mA units then your reading would only be accurate to ±0·5 mA, that is ± half a scale division and should be quoted as 2·5±0·5 mA. It would be much better to use a 0–5 mA meter for such a reading since the scale would probably be calibrated in 0·2 mA units and you could quote your reading as 2·5±0·1 mA.

Another example is the use of a micrometer screw gauge to measure the diameter of a wire. Such gauges are calibrated in 0·01 mm divisions on their drum scale. Suppose the reading taken was as shown in Fig. 3.1. The reading is obviously nearer 3·50 mm than 3·49 mm so we would quote it as 3·500±0·005 mm.

When using a stop watch the user's reaction time (of the order of 0·2 s for most people) is comparable to the 'action' of the watch which is usually 0·1 or 0·2 s. In this case the instrument error will be concealed by the user's error. Some laboratory stop clocks however have a 0·25 s 'action' so when using these the error will be ±0·25 s on any timings. We do not use ± half the smallest scale division in this case since the action of the seconds hand is an intermittent one.

Combining errors

In physics the final result is frequently a combination (sums, differences, products, etc.) of a number of readings, quite often of totally different quantities. Assuming we can estimate the error for each type of reading what will be the error in the final result? In other words how do individual errors combine when placed in a formula? Consider a simple example. We measure the length of an object with a meter rule calibrated in mm. (The length might be the difference in mercury levels h in the two arms of a manometer as shown in Fig. 3.2).

To obtain h we have to subtract one reading from the other and,

$$h = R_2 - R_1$$

but R_2 was made to an accuracy of ±0·5 mm, similarly R_1 is accurate to ±0·5 mm. Therefore the actual value of h is given by,

$$h \pm \Delta h = (R_2 \pm \Delta R_2) - (R_1 \pm \Delta R_1)$$

$$h \pm \Delta h = (R_2 \pm 0·5 \text{ mm}) - (R_1 \pm 0·5 \text{ mm})$$

Is the error in h the sum of the errors in R_1 and R_2, or the difference, or what? If we take the worst possible case with R_2 being read too high and R_1 being read too low

$$\Delta R_1 = +0·5 \text{ mm}$$

and

$$\Delta R_2 = -0·5 \text{ mm}$$

Therefore

$$\Delta h = +1·0 \text{ mm}$$

Similarly if R_1 was read too low and R_2 was read too high

$$\Delta R_1 = -0·5 \text{ mm}$$

and

$$\Delta R_2 = +0·5 \text{ mm}$$

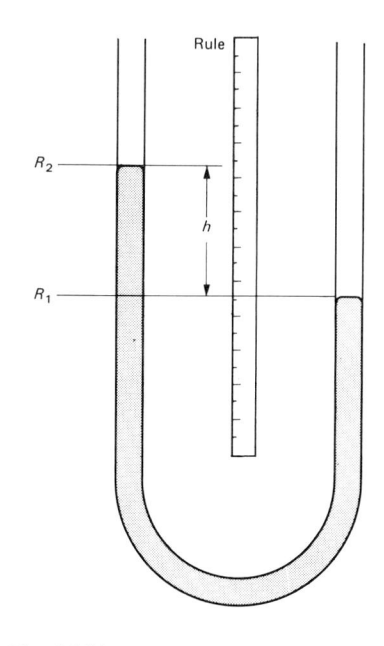

Fig. 3.2 Mercury manometer.

Therefore $\Delta h = -1.0$ mm

Hence the worst situation is that,

$$\Delta h = \pm(\Delta R_1 + \Delta R_2) = \pm 1.0 \text{ mm}$$

That is, although R_1 is subtracted from R_2 to get h, the worst possible error is obtained by adding the individual errors. The same situation would occur if R_1 and R_2 had to be added to get the final result. The worst possible error would still be obtained by adding the individual errors ΔR_1 and ΔR_2. There is also the possibility that R_1 and R_2 were both read high or both read low. This gives,

$$\Delta h = +0.5 \text{ mm} - (+0.5 \text{ mm}) = 0$$

or $\Delta h = -0.5 \text{ mm} - (-0.5 \text{ mm}) = 0$

This is the best possible situation with errors completely cancelling.

In practice we try to work with the probable error rather than the worst or best possible error. Statistics tell us that the probable error will be somewhere between these two but it is not simply their average.

The possible error $\Delta h = \pm(\Delta R_1 + \Delta R_2)$

but the probable error is given by

$$\Delta h = \pm[(\Delta R_1)^2 + (\Delta R_2)^2]^{\frac{1}{2}}$$

which is less than $\Delta R_1 + \Delta R_2$.

This becomes clearer when we insert figures.

Possible error $\Delta h = \pm(0.5 + 0.5) = \pm 1.0$ mm

Probable error $\Delta h = \pm(0.5^2 + 0.5^2)^{\frac{1}{2}}$
$= \pm(0.25 + 0.25)^{\frac{1}{2}} = \pm(0.5)^{\frac{1}{2}} = \pm 0.71$ mm

These ideas can be applied to any sum or difference situation. If a result X is due to the addition and subtraction of a number of results R_1, R_2, R_3, etc. then,

$$X = (R_1 - R_2 - R_3 + R_4 \text{ etc.})$$

Possible error $\Delta X = \pm(\Delta R_1 + \Delta R_2 + \Delta R_3 + \Delta R_4 + \ldots)$

Probable error $\Delta X = \pm[(\Delta R_1)^2 + (\Delta R_2)^2 + (\Delta R_3)^2 + (\Delta R_4)^2 + \ldots]^{\frac{1}{2}}$

We now have to consider how to combine the errors when two or more quantities multiply or divide to give the final result. It is not so obvious in this case what physically happens to the errors when the results are combined so we will rely on the mathematics. Suppose our final result X is the product of two measurements Y and Z. That is $X = YZ$.

Then $X \pm \Delta X = (Y \pm \Delta Y)(Z \pm \Delta Z)$

Multiplying out we get,

$$X \pm \Delta X = YZ \pm Y\Delta Z \pm Z\Delta Y \pm \Delta Y \Delta Z$$

We ignore the last term since it is a product of two small quantities and since $X = YZ$ we can cancel these terms. This leaves,

$$\Delta X = \pm Y\Delta Z \pm Z\Delta Y$$

Dividing both sides by YZ,

$$\frac{\Delta X}{YZ} = \frac{\Delta X}{X} = \pm \frac{\Delta Z}{Z} \pm \frac{\Delta Y}{Y}$$

This shows that the fractional (or percentage) error in X has a worst possible value of the sum of the fractional errors in Y and Z. The probable fractional error in X is given by,

$$\pm \left[\left(\frac{\Delta Y}{Y}\right)^2 + \left(\frac{\Delta Z}{Z}\right)^2 \right]^{\frac{1}{2}}$$

just as when we added results in the previous example.

It is quite easy to show that if $X = Y/Z$ or $X = Z/Y$ we still get the same possible and probable fractional errors for X as before. That is,

$$\frac{\Delta X}{X} = \pm \left(\frac{\Delta Y}{Y} + \frac{\Delta Z}{Z}\right) \qquad \text{possible}$$

$$\frac{\Delta X}{X} = \pm \left[\left(\frac{\Delta Y}{Y}\right)^2 + \left(\frac{\Delta Z}{Z}\right)^2 \right]^{\frac{1}{2}} \qquad \text{probable}$$

If three or more terms are involved in the equation we can extend the probable or possible error equation to account for the errors in them. For example if,

$$X = YZ/VW$$

$$\frac{\Delta X}{X} = \pm \left[\left(\frac{\Delta Y}{Y}\right)^2 + \left(\frac{\Delta Z}{Z}\right)^2 + \left(\frac{\Delta V}{V}\right)^2 + \left(\frac{\Delta W}{W}\right)^2 \right]^{\frac{1}{2}}$$

In fact any number of terms can be handled in this way.

A simple example of the above type of error combination occurs when you compare two resistors using a potentiometer. The ratio of the two resistances $R_1/R_2 = l_1/l_2$ where l_1 and l_2 are the two appropriate balance lengths on the potentiometer wire. These can be measured to ± 0.5 mm. Suppose they are $l_1 = 50.7$ cm, $l_2 = 41.3$ cm and R_2 is a standard $2\,\Omega$ resistor. Then,

$$R_1 = \frac{l_1}{l_2} R_2 = \frac{50.7}{41.3} \times 2.0 = 2.46\,\Omega$$

The probable fractional error,

$$\frac{\Delta R_1}{R_1} = \pm \left[\left(\frac{\Delta l_1}{l_1}\right)^2 + \left(\frac{\Delta l_2}{l_2}\right)^2 + \left(\frac{\Delta R_2}{R_2}\right)^2 \right]^{\frac{1}{2}}$$

As R_2 is a standard resistor we can assume that ΔR_2 is very small so we neglect it. This gives,

$$\frac{\Delta R_1}{R_1} = \pm \left[\left(\frac{0.5}{507}\right)^2 + \left(\frac{0.5}{413}\right)^2 \right]^{\frac{1}{2}} = \pm [0.973 \times 10^{-6} + 1.470 \times 10^{-6}]^{\frac{1}{2}}$$

$$\frac{\Delta R_1}{R_1} = \pm \sqrt{(2 \cdot 44)} \times 10^{-3} = \pm 1 \cdot 56 \times 10^{-3}$$

$$\Delta R_1 = \pm 2 \cdot 46 \times 1 \cdot 56 \times 10^{-3} = \pm 3 \cdot 83 \times 10^{-3}\ \Omega$$

$$\therefore R_1 = 2 \cdot 46 \pm 3 \cdot 83 \times 10^{-3}\ \Omega$$

Notice that since all measurements were made to three significant figures in the experiment only three significant figures have been used in the calculations. We are not justified in using more than three figures in the calculations since the original measurements were only made to that accuracy.

One other problem occurs when combining errors. What happens to the errors if the results to be combined have a power other than unity? That is if $X = Z^n$ what is the error in X? This problem can be solved by the use of the binomial theorem.

$$X + \Delta X = (Z + \Delta Z)^n = Z^n(1 + \Delta Z/Z)^n$$

If we expand the bracket binomially we get

$$X + \Delta X = Z^n \left[1 + n\frac{\Delta Z}{Z} + \frac{n(n-1)}{2!}\left(\frac{\Delta Z}{Z}\right)^2 + \frac{n(n-1)(n-2)}{3!}\left(\frac{\Delta Z}{Z}\right)^3 + \ldots \right]$$

Ignoring all powers of ΔZ greater than one (since ΔZ is small compared with Z) we get,

$$X + \Delta X = Z^n \left[1 + n\frac{\Delta Z}{Z} \right] = Z^n + n\Delta Z . Z^{n-1}$$

Since $X = Z^n$ this gives,

$$\Delta X = n\Delta Z . Z^{n-1}$$

and

$$\frac{\Delta X}{X} = n\frac{\Delta Z}{Z}$$

Hence the general rule is that if a quantity is raised to a power (positive, negative or fractional) in a formula the fractional error in that quantity is multiplied by the power number. This means that if a quantity appears with a high power number in a formula it is particularly important to try to measure that quantity to a high accuracy since the fractional error due to it will be multiplied by the power number in the error formula. A good example of this situation is in Poiseuille's formula for laminar flow of a liquid through a tube. This states,

$$\text{Volume flowing per second } V = \frac{\pi p a^4}{8 \zeta l}$$

where p is the pressure difference across the ends of the tube, a is its radius, ζ the coefficient of viscosity of the liquid and l the length of the tube. The formula is used to deduce ζ.

$$\zeta = \frac{\pi p a^4}{8 V l}$$

This gives a possible fractional error in ζ of,

$$\frac{\Delta \zeta}{\zeta} = \pm \left[\frac{\Delta p}{p} + \frac{4\Delta a}{a} + \frac{\Delta V}{V} + \frac{\Delta l}{l} \right]$$

and a probable error of,

$$\frac{\Delta \zeta}{\zeta} = \pm \left[\left(\frac{\Delta p}{p}\right)^2 + \left(\frac{4\Delta a}{a}\right)^2 + \left(\frac{\Delta V}{V}\right)^2 + \left(\frac{\Delta l}{l}\right)^2 \right]^{\frac{1}{2}}$$

(π is not involved since it is a pure number and not a measured quantity).

As an example of the use of the above equation consider a capillary tube of length 200 mm and diameter 1 mm. A pressure difference of 5 cm of water (measured by a manometer) produces a flow of water of 0·96 cm^3 s^{-1}.

The pressure $p = \rho g h$ where h is the head on the manometer (5 cm). Therefore,

$$\frac{\Delta p}{p} = \frac{\Delta h}{h}$$

if we assume ρ and g are very accurately known, $\Delta h = \pm 1$ mm (worst possible error in measurement. See page 38).

Therefore $\quad \dfrac{\Delta p}{p} = \pm \dfrac{1 \cdot 0}{50} = \pm 0 \cdot 02$

a is measured with a travelling microscope with a vernier accurate to $\pm 0 \cdot 010$ mm. This gives a worst possible error of $\pm 0 \cdot 020$ mm for a (and a probable value of 0·014 mm. See page 38).

Therefore $\quad \dfrac{\Delta a}{a} = \pm 0 \cdot 02$ and $4 \dfrac{\Delta a}{a} = \pm 0 \cdot 08$

$l = 200$ mm and if measured with the same travelling microscope to accuracy $\pm 0 \cdot 01$ mm the worst possible error is $\pm 0 \cdot 02$ mm

$$\frac{\Delta l}{l} = \pm \frac{0 \cdot 02}{200} = \pm 10^{-4}$$

We can neglect this as it is so small compared with the other fractional errors (in fact it would be quite satisfactory to measure l with a metre rule since this would only give

$$\frac{\Delta l}{l} = \pm \frac{2 \text{ mm}}{200 \text{ mm}} = \pm 0 \cdot 01).$$

By combining the volume measurement and timing errors the worst value of ΔV would be $\pm 0 \cdot 009$ cm^3 s^{-1} so that,

$$\frac{\Delta V}{V} = \pm \frac{0 \cdot 009}{0 \cdot 96} = \pm 0 \cdot 0095$$

Combining the errors to get the probable fractional error we have,

$$\frac{\Delta \zeta}{\zeta} = \pm [(0 \cdot 02)^2 + (0 \cdot 08)^2 + (10^{-4})^2 + (0 \cdot 0095)^2]^{\frac{1}{2}}$$

$$= \pm [0 \cdot 0004 + 0 \cdot 0064 + 0 \cdot 00009]^{\frac{1}{2}} = \pm 0 \cdot 081$$

(the worst possible value is $\pm 0 \cdot 11$).

The actual value of ζ turns out to be 0·001 SI units so that $\zeta = 0.001 \pm 0.000081$ SI units.

This example is a complicated one. We simplified slightly by assuming worst errors instead of probable in calculating the individual errors and then combined them to get the final probable error. The fact that $4\Delta a/a$ contributed most of the final error is significant in two ways. It shows the necessity for accurate measurements where large power numbers are involved, and it is so large compared with the other fractional errors that for practical purposes they can be neglected. Such neglect would lead to ± 0.080 for $\Delta\zeta/\zeta$ instead of the probable ± 0.081.

Frequently in physics experiments this sort of situation occurs and it is worth spending a little time examining the results to find the dominant error. It may then be possible to simplify the error estimation by only using this dominant value. It may also be possible to re-design the equipment to reduce the dominant error to the same level as the others.

Significant figures

When writing down a result the number of significant figures you use should be a guide to the accuracy of the measurement. For example if the diameter of a wire is measured to an accuracy of ± 0.1 mm and is found to lie between 2·45 mm and 2·55 mm the diameter should be quoted as 2·5 mm and not 2·50 mm. The last zero would imply 0·01 mm accuracy. If this value of 2·5 mm was quoted in micrometres (μm) it could be written as 2500 μm. This would imply that the reading was accurate to 1 μm which it certainly is not. The correct way to write the value in μm is 2.5×10^3 μm and if it could be made to 1 μm accuracy then 2.500×10^3 μm would be the correct expression. Again if the reading was expressed in metres it should be written as 0·0025 m not 0·00250 m.

Sometimes in calculations extra significant figures arise and these should be corrected back to the original number of significant figures. This saves time in the calculation and such figures have no physical significance anyway as they are below the limits of accuracy of the original readings.

As an example consider the addition of the currents at the junction shown in Fig. 3.3. The values of currents I_1, I_2 and I_3 are 0·37 A, 2 A and 1·4 A.

$$I = I_1 + I_2 + I_3 = 3.77 \text{ A}$$

We are only justified in quoting I as 4 A since I_2 is only known to the nearest ampere (only one significant figure was quoted).

Similarly when we calculate the volume of a corridor of length 12·76 m, width 1·45 m and height 3·24 m we obtain

$$\text{volume} = 1.45 \times 3.24 \times 12.76 = 59.94648 \text{ m}^3$$

Since the height and width were only measured to three significant figures we are only justified in quoting the result (volume) to this accuracy as 60·0 m³.

In general then the accuracy of a result is no better (and is usually worse) than that of the least accurate quantity in it.

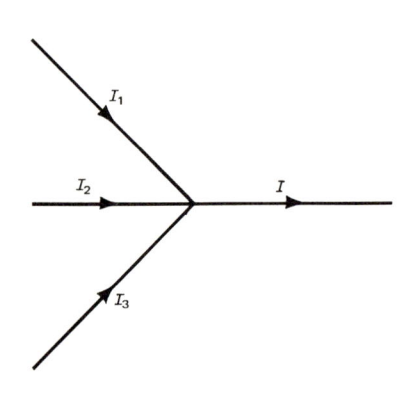

Fig. 3.3 Currents meeting at a junction.

A few hints on calculating

When averaging a large number of results it is often easier to use a false mean method to avoid lengthy additions. This is best shown by an example. Suppose we have five values of the diameter of a wire taken at different points along its length. These are 0·347, 0·349, 0·351, 0·346 and 0·345 mm. We choose a false mean, say 0·346, and add the differences from this mean,

$$+0·001 + 0·003 + 0·005 + 0 - 0·001 = +0·008$$

We divide by the number of results which is 5 and obtain +0·0016. Then the true mean is 0·346 + 0·0016 = 0·348 mm.

Another useful hint is that when a number of readings of the same quantity have to be put into a formula and the final result averaged it saves time if the readings are averaged before being put into the formula. In this way the formula need only be evaluated once. For example in the Young's Modulus formula for a wire,

$$E = \frac{\text{Load}}{\pi d^2/4} \bigg/ \frac{\text{Extension}}{\text{Natural Length}}$$

where d is the diameter of the wire and is measured in a number of places along the wire. You would not insert each diameter value into the formula and then average the value of E but rather insert an averaged value of d into the formula and perform the calculation for E once.

Many students when performing calculations on experimental results produce ridiculous results. That is, ones which are obviously physically very unlikely. You should always question the results of experimental calculations on the basis of 'do they make physical sense?' A pocket set of physical tables is useful here although a comprehensive set of tables should always be available in your laboratory. Small books of mathematical tables with condensed physical tables are freely available and are well worth purchasing.

This brings us to the final point—log tables, slide rule or computer? Four or five figure logs are quite accurate enough for all work in physics at this level but using them is a fairly slow process. A slide rule gives four figure accuracy at one end but only three figure accuracy at the other. Nevertheless for your purposes it is usually accurate enough and in a practised hand is very much quicker than using tables. Most slide rules carry a range of trigonometric function scales, squares, reciprocals, etc. and can act as an almost complete substitute for the usual mathematical tables. To make the best use of the slide rule you need to develop speed and accuracy with it. For this there is no substitute for practice. Use the manufacturer's booklet, ask for demonstrations from your teacher and get down to hard use of the device on practical problems.

Many schools and colleges have data links to computer centres. If you have had some programming training it may be possible to write programmes for some of the problems you meet in your physics practical work. This is probably not worth while for routine laboratory experiments but may be useful for project work always assuming that you have enough time (and money) allocation.

Chapter 4 The Experimental Tests

Introduction

You will probably have found that you already knew a great deal of the previous sections on straight line graphs, graph plotting and so on. This is material which is fairly easy to pick up as you go along when doing physics practical work but it is important to have a systematic guide to all aspects of graph plotting and that is what the previous sections are designed to provide. They cover all that you need at Advanced level or OND standard and in fact almost all that you would need on a physics degree course (where a little extra work on theory of errors would be required).

The stage has now been reached where all the ideas mentioned previously will be applied to a series of experimental situations. As you work through these you will find that you are eventually applying the basic techniques of good graph drawing, choice of scales, etc. automatically and can concentrate on the interpretation of the graph.

The tests fall into three main groups which merge into each other. In the first group (Test 1 to Test 6) you are mainly being tested on technique in drawing graphs. That is, choice of scale, origins, labelling, best straight line or curve and so on. The questions on the use of the graph are very straightforward and you should find them quite easy. Do not be tempted to ignore this section on the grounds that it is too easy. It is meant to get you into automatic good habits when drawing and interpreting simple graphs. Because they are made very simple the actual experiments may seem rather contrived and artificial but remember that they are primarily exercises at this stage.

The next group (up to Test 16) involve progressively harder laboratory situations but the actual graphs are no more difficult to draw than the earlier ones and you should be able to do them more quickly now. The questions concerning the graphs will require a lot more thought and in the later tests are of the standard you are likely to meet in GCE Advanced level examination.

The last group comprise situations where GCE Advanced level/OND standard physics has been applied to meet 'real' situations. That is actual problems met inside and outside the laboratory rather than teaching experiments where the results are fairly predictable. If you have worked through the previous tests conscientiously these real situations should not frighten you—in fact you should find it exciting to see how your knowledge can be used to solve real problems. This after all is what trained scientists and engineers do throughout their working lives. This is the type of test which you will meet in your GCE Advanced level examination and which you are expected to finish in one and a half hours.

Allow yourself one and a half hours for each of the tests. You may find you do not need this time for some of the early ones but with the later ones you certainly will.

All except the last four tests have brief notes indicating what types of skill they are designed to test and some of the tests tell you where you can find guidance in the previous sections.

You will probably find it helpful to read the introduction again after reading through the whole of the test. An error analysis is not required in the tests but you should remember the points about significant figures mentioned on page 42.

Full answers and comments on the questions together with the relevant graph or graphs are provided in Appendix 1. To some of the questions there is no definite single answer but the relative merits of the various possibilities will be discussed. Do try to work through the tests without looking at the appendix first. Ask for guidance from your teacher as you do them if you feel you need it, invite his comments at the end and then check your answers etc. with the guide in the appendix.

Test One

Measurement of *g* by timing

This simple experiment is one which you may have done in your Ordinary level physics. It enables a direct measurement of the acceleration due to gravity *g* to be made. This test involves the choice of correct variables (see page 9) and good drawing techniques (pages 29–33). A tangent to the student's curve is required and hints on drawing tangents are given on pages 34 and 35.

Test 1

A student was asked to investigate how the time of free fall of a ball bearing depended on the distance fallen and hence to deduce a value for *g*, the acceleration due to gravity. The apparatus used enables the time of the fall of the ball bearing to be measured directly with an electrical timer. The ball is held at *A* by a solenoid. Breaking the circuit of the solenoid releases the ball and starts the timer. When the ball hits the flap at *B* it breaks another circuit and stops the timer. See Fig. 4.1(a). The distance *h* can be varied over a range 0 to 1·5 m and the timer is accurate to 0·005 s. The student obtained the results shown in Table 4.1.

Theory indicates that *h* is related to time *t* by,

$$h = \tfrac{1}{2}gt^2$$

Fig. 4.1(a) Measurement of '*g*' by timing.

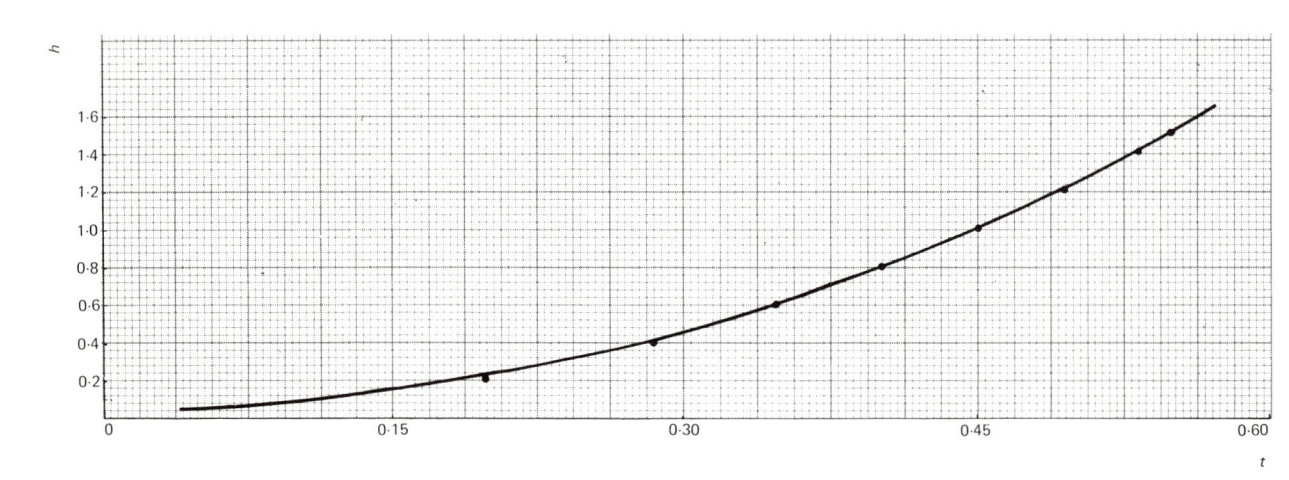

Fig. 4.1(b).

Distance h, (m)	Time t, (s)
0·20	0·200
0·40	0·285
0·60	0·350
0·80	0·400
1·00	0·450
1·20	0·495
1·40	0·535
1·50	0·550

Table 4.1.

The student plotted the graph of h against t as shown in Fig. 4.1(b) but could get no further.

Answer the following questions:

(1) Is this the correct graph to plot in order to verify $h = \frac{1}{2}gt^2$? If not, what graph should be plotted?

(2) There are five other bad features to this graph. List them.

(3) Plot the correct graph avoiding the bad features above and measure its slope. Hence deduce the value of g.

(4) Using the student's graph, measure the slope at $t = 0·5$ s. What does this slope represent?

Test Two

Measurement of the height of the ceiling using a simple pendulum

Test 2

Theory

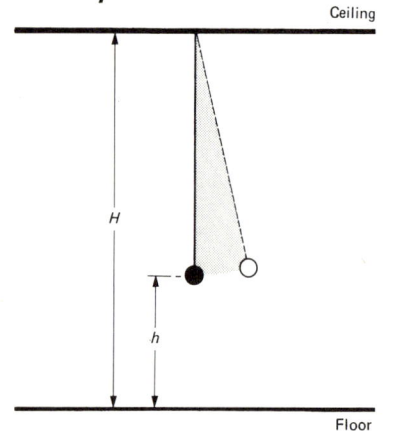

Fig. 4.2 Height of the ceiling.

Height h of Bob above floor, (m)	Time for 50 oscillations, (s)
0·40	155·3
0·60	148·8
0·80	142·2
1·00	134·0
1·20	127·4
1·40	119·2
1·60	110·5

Table 4.2.

This involves a rather artificial way of measuring the height of the ceiling. Like the previous problem it tests your ability to draw well and to choose the correct variables to plot. In addition this time you have the problem of choice of origins since intercepts are involved (see pages 13-18 on the theory of the straight line graph and on the measurement of intercepts with true or false origins).

As an examination exercise a student was presented with a stop watch, two metre rules and a simple pendulum suspended from a ceiling and was asked to measure the ceiling height indirectly. He set the pendulum swinging through a small angle and measured the period of oscillation for different lengths of the pendulum. As he was unable to measure the length of the pendulum directly he measured the height of the centre of the pendulum bob above the floor. He obtained the results shown in Table 4.2.

The period T of a simple pendulum of length l is given by

$$T = 2\pi \sqrt{\frac{l}{g}}$$

where g is the acceleration due to gravity.

But $l = H - h$ where H is the height of the ceiling, and h is the height of the centre of the pendulum bob above the floor. See Fig. 4.2.

Therefore
$$T = 2\pi \sqrt{\frac{H-h}{g}}$$

Using the student's results plot a suitable graph and use it to find the height of the ceiling H from the two intercepts. You will need to assume that g is 9·8 ms^{-2}. (Note that g could be obtained from the slope of the graph).

Having obtained your values for H answer the following questions:

(1) Which value of H do you consider the least accurate? Give reasons for your choice and explain how the accuracy could have been improved.
(2) Why was the bob set swinging through a small angle?
(3) Why was h measured to the centre of the bob?
(4) Why was the complete number of oscillations chosen to be large?
(5) Can you see any advantage in measuring the height of the ceiling in this way?

Test Three

An experiment involving the tuning of sonometer wires

This exercise was set some years ago in an GCE Advanced level practical examination. It leads to no profound results and is really only an exercise in plotting. The value of the slope obtained acts as a check on the accuracy with which the tuning was done and the graph plotted. Once again your drawing ability will be tested. No intercepts are involved this time.

M_A (fixed) = 4·5 kg
l_B (fixed) = 0·460 m

M_B, (kg)	l_A, (m)
4·0	0·500
4·5	0·471
5·0	0·452
5·5	0·434
6·0	0·420
6·5	0·400
7·0	0·387
7·5	0·377
8·0	0·364
8·5	0·355

Table 4.3.

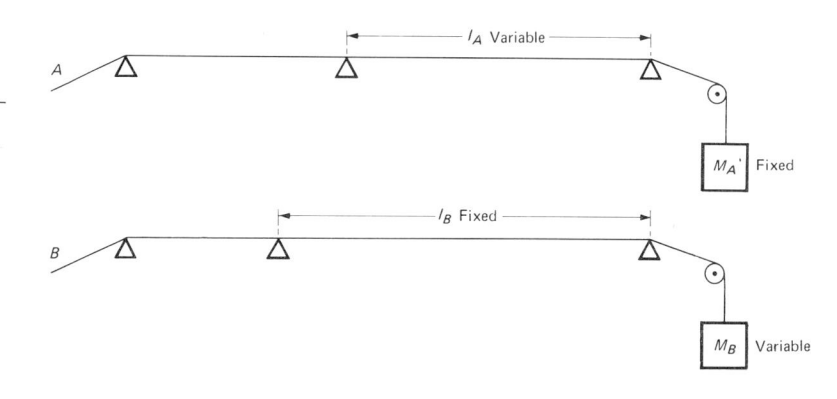

Fig. 4.3 Tuning sonometer wires.

Test 3

Two identical sonometer wires A and B, made of steel, were positioned on the same sound box side by side. See Fig. 4.3. A load M_A was applied to A and adjusted until a good note was obtained. M_A was kept fixed at this value throughout the experiment. A load M_B was applied to B until a fixed length l_B of B gave the same note (frequency) as a length l_A of A. M_B was varied and the corresponding lengths l_A of A were found so that the note from A was in unison with the note from the fixed length of B. The results shown in Table 4.3 were obtained.

Using these results plot a graph with M_B^{-1} as ordinate against l_A^2 as abscissa. Measure the slope S of the graph and calculate the value of $Sl_B^2 M_A$.

Theory

The fundamental frequency f_0 of a stretched wire is given by,

$$f_0 = \frac{1}{2l}\sqrt{\frac{T}{m}}$$

where l is the length of the wire, T is the tension and m is the mass per unit length of the wire.

When tuned A and B have the same frequency hence,

$$\frac{1}{2l_A}\sqrt{\frac{M_A g}{m}} = \frac{1}{2l_B}\sqrt{\frac{M_B g}{m}}$$

where g is the acceleration due to gravity. This gives,

$$\frac{M_A}{l_A^2} = \frac{M_B}{l_B^2} \quad \text{or} \quad \frac{1}{M_B} = \left(\frac{1}{M_A l_B^2}\right) l_A^2$$

Hence plotting M_B^{-1} as ordinate against l_A^2 as abscissa should give a straight line graph of slope

$$S = \frac{1}{M_A l_B^2}$$

Hence $S l_B^2 M_A$ should be unity. This acts as a check on the accuracy of the tuning and of the plotting of the graph.

Answer the following questions:

(1) The maximum usable lengths of wires A and B were 0·9 m and the maximum load each could carry was 12·0 kg. With l_B set at 0·460 m and M_A fixed at 4·5 kg find the range of variation of l_A and the corresponding range of M_B which can be produced.

(2) Can you suggest any parts of the graph where extra readings might have been taken?

(3) If a brass wire of identical dimensions was substituted for the steel wire B and the experiment repeated using the same loads M_B how would the values of l_A be affected? (Density of brass = 1·1 times density of steel). If the breaking stress is half that of steel, what effect would this have on the possible range of values of l_A?

(4) If in the original experiment the constant load was completely immersed in water explain how l_A would have to be varied to obtain unison again.

Test Four

Determination of focal length of a convex lens by plotting distance between object and image against object distance

This test involves plotting a hyperbola and measuring the position of its minimum. You will have to be particularly careful to choose the horizontal scale sensibly otherwise you will find the curve difficult to draw and the minimum difficult to judge. As you can see from the sketch graph (Fig. 4.4(a)) you are required to draw the asymptotes of the hyperbola. These are tangents to the hyperbola at infinity but you will find them fairly easy to judge with this particular curve. There is no need to use a plane mirror or the other method mentioned on page 35.

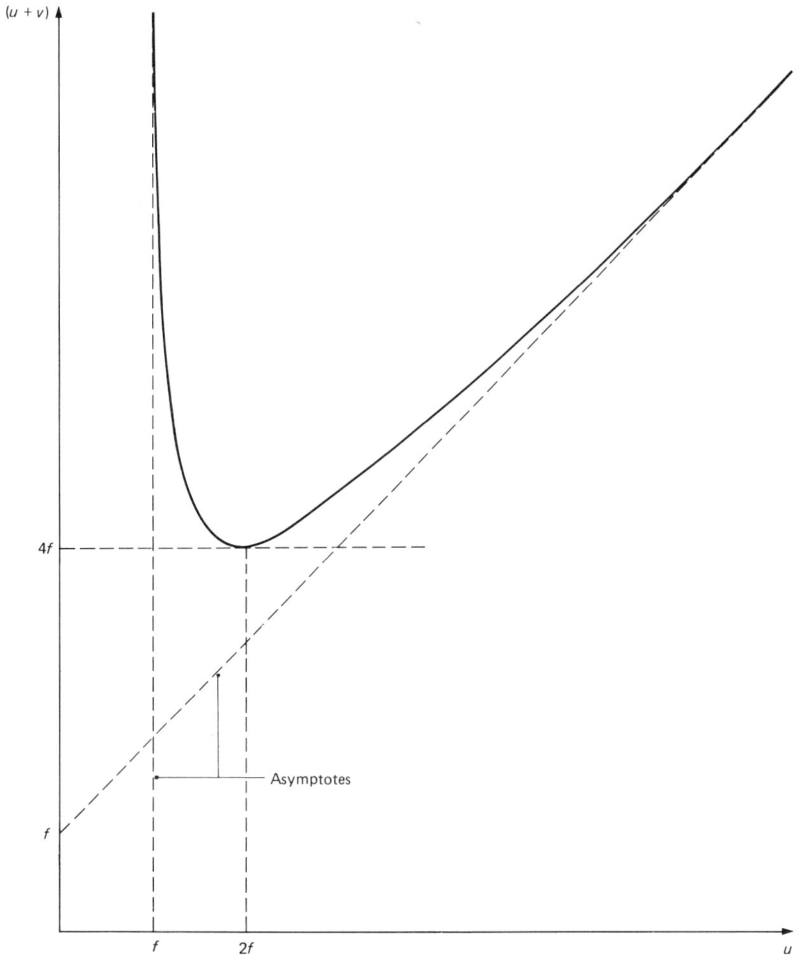

Fig. 4.4(a) Graph of $(u + v)$ against u.

Object Distance u, (cm)	Image Distance v, (cm)
11·0	89·0
12·0	52·2
13·0	40·7
14·0	34·0
15·0	29·0
16·0	26·8
17·0	24·7
18·0	23·0
19·0	21·6
20·0	20·6
21·0	19·6
22·0	19·2
25·0	17·4
27·0	16·3
30·0	15·7
35·0	14·6
40·0	14·0
45·0	13·8
50·0	13·4
55·0	13·2
60·0	12·8

Table 4.4.

Fig. 4.4(b) Determination of focal length.

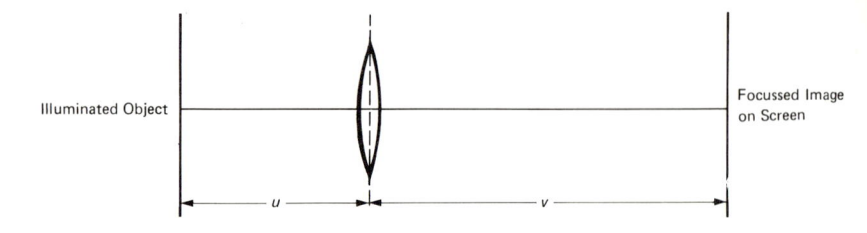

Test 4

The object was placed at various distances u from the lens and the image distance v was found in each case. See Fig. 4.4(b). The results shown in Table 4.4 were obtained. Using these results plot a graph of $(u+v)$ as ordinate against u as abscissa. The form of the graph is shown in Fig. 4.4(a).

Theory indicates that the graph is a rectangular hyperbola having as asymptotes lines whose equations are $u = f$ and $(u+v) = u+f$. Use of calculus shows that the minimum of the graph occurs at $u = 2f$ and $(u+v) = 4f$. There are therefore four ways of obtaining the focal length f from the graph. Obtain these four values from your graph and then answer the following questions:

(1) In view of the fact that the experimenter had a 1·5 m optical bench, do you consider he made the best possible use of it?

(2) Are there any regions of the graph where you consider he should have taken more readings? If so, why?

(3) In view of the answers you have given above, which of your four values for f do you consider the most reliable? Explain your reasoning.

(4) What would you observe if the screen is placed so that the distance between the object and the screen is just less than $4f$?

Test Five

Cantilever experiment

This simple experiment is another which has been set in the past as an Advanced level practical examination. It is an exercise in plotting a log-log graph and if you need help in this refer to pages 18–21. In fact although the results given to you require no bar number logs the question at the end does refer to such a log.

The constant K in the equation $D = KL^n$ depends on the width and thickness of the ruler and also on the value of the Young's Modulus for the ruler material. The equation only holds for small deflections.

The best way to find K is to use false origins and calculate $\log_{10} K$ using the coordinates of a point on the graph but be careful when anti-logging. You would find that any attempt to use zero origins would involve you in scale difficulties.

Test 5

A light wooden uniform lath (metre rule) was clamped to the surface of a bench so that a length L of the lath was overhanging the edge. The end of the lath was loaded with a mass and the depression D produced at the loaded end was measured. (See Fig. 4.5). Values of D were obtained for different lengths L.

Assuming that $D = KL^n$, where K and n are constants, draw a suitable graph using the results shown in Table 4.5 to determine n and K.

Use the graph to find the value of L for $D = 0.5$ mm.

Depression D, (mm)	Length L, (mm)
2·0	200
6·0	300
13·0	400
28·0	500
49·0	600
75·0	700
109·0	800

Table 4.5.

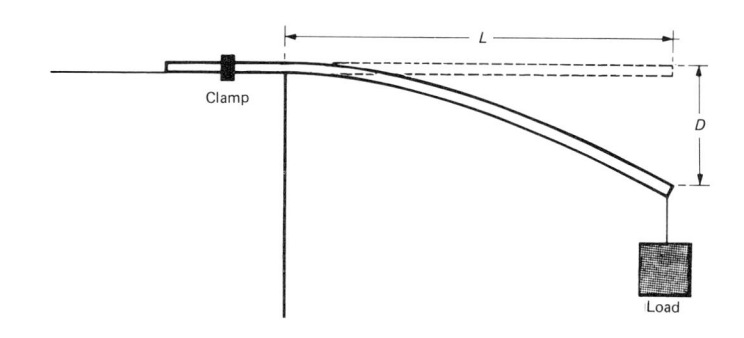

Fig. 4.5 Cantilever experiment.

Test Six

Dependence of period on length for a simple pendulum

Test 6

This test is a follow through to the previous one in that it involves a log-log graph with bar numbers. The axes should be set out as shown in Fig. 1.12. As it is an exercise do not avoid the bar numbers by converting the values of l to mm or cm. Again an intercept has to be measured and it is probably best in this case to use true zero origins.

The periodic time T for a simple pendulum of length l is given by,

$$T = 2\pi \sqrt{\frac{l}{g}}$$

where g is the acceleration due to gravity.

In an experiment to determine the dependence of T on l in the formula for the period of a simple pendulum a student obtained the set of results shown in Table 4.6.

Let $T = kl^n$ where k is a constant. Taking logs we obtain,

$$\log_{10} T = n \log_{10} l + \log_{10} k$$

Plot a suitable graph to obtain values for n and k. Compare these values with those obtained from the formula

$$T = 2\pi \sqrt{\frac{l}{g}} \quad \text{(Use } g = 9.8 \text{ ms}^{-2}\text{)}$$

The procedure of assuming that T is only dependent on l in some way, of writing $T = kl^n$ and then finding n and k graphically is a very simple example of the technique mentioned on page 24. Although the values of n and k are known in this example, in actual experimental situations the form of the dependence of one variable on another may not be known. The form (value of n) can be found by this log-log method.

Period T, (s)	Length of pendulum l, (m)
1·10	0·3
1·42	0·5
1·68	0·7
1·90	0·9
2·11	1·1
2·29	1·3
2·46	1·5
2·62	1·7

Table 4.6.

Test Seven

The power delivered to a load resistor by a cell

This test involves drawing a curve and measuring its maximum. You will find it slightly easier to draw than the curve in Test Four but the questions concerning it are correspondingly harder. As in Test Four the choice of horizontal scale will determine the shape of the curve and the ease with which you can draw it. You can only determine the best choice of scale by trying it.

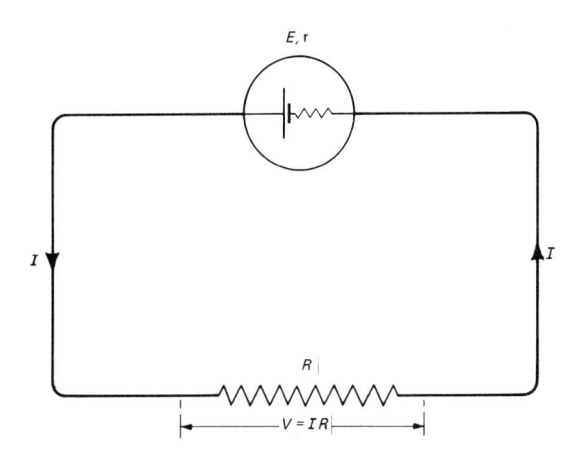

Fig. 4.7(a) Load across a cell.

When a load resistance R is connected across the terminals of a cell of e.m.f. E and internal resistance r, a current I will flow and a terminal potential difference $V = IR$ will be set up across it (consequence of Ohm's law). See Fig. 4.7(a). It is found that the terminal potential difference V is always less than the e.m.f. of the cell by a factor which depends on both R and r. This dependence is given by,

$$V = \frac{R}{(R+r)} \cdot E$$

If R is increased $V \to E$ and $V = E$ when $R = \infty$. That is, the open circuit condition.

Conversely if $R \to 0$ then $V \to 0$ also

In the first case as $R \to \infty$ then $I \to 0$

In the second case as $R \to 0$ then I becomes very large.

The power IV in the load is of importance in many practical instances and it is not obvious from the above how the power $P = IV$ varies as R is varied from zero towards infinity.

To measure such a variation, a student set up a simple circuit as shown in Fig. 4.7(b) using a very high resistance voltmeter whose

Test 7

Resistance R, (Ω)	Current I, (A)	Potential difference V, (V)
0		
1·0	0·250	0·25
2·0	0·219	0·43
3·0	0·188	0·56
4·0	0·162	0·67
5·0	0·150	0·75
6·0	0·136	0·82
7·0	0·125	0·88
8·0	0·116	0·92
9·0	0·107	0·97
10·0	0·100	1·00
12·0	0·090	1·06
15·0	0·075	1·12
20·0	0·060	1·20

Table 4.7.

Fig. 4.7(b) The circuit.

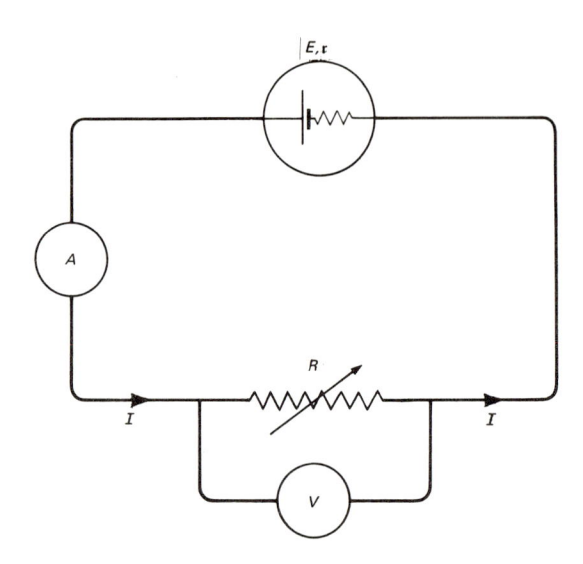

shunting effect on the load resistor is negligible. The supply is a large dry cell of e.m.f. = 1·5 V and 5 ohm internal resistance. He set R at various values and recorded I and V as shown in Table 4.7. Using these results, plot a graph of power IV against R and answer the following questions:

(1) Why have no values of I and V for R = 0 been shown in the above set of results?

(2) In view of the way the values of I and V have been recorded, comment on the accuracy and probable range of the ammeter and voltmeter used.

(3) From your graph, measure the maximum power obtained. At what value of R does this occur?

(4) Using $$V = \frac{R}{(R+r)} \cdot E \quad \text{and} \quad I = \frac{V}{R}$$

we can express the power,

$$P = IV = \frac{V^2}{R} = \frac{R}{(R+r)^2} \cdot E^2$$

Calculate the value of P when R = r. Does this coincide with the value deduced from your graph in question 3?

(5) Using $$P = \frac{R}{(R+r)^2} \cdot E^2$$

what would the value of P become if,

(a) R is very large but not infinite?
(b) R → 0?

Are these results confirmed by the trend of your graph?

(6) What is the general conclusion to be drawn from question 4? Would you expect this idea to be applicable to other forms of electrical power supply such as the mains, transformers, oscillators, etc.?

Test Eight

Resistance–temperature characteristics

This test involves a certain amount of scientific detective work concerning the nature of an electronic component. You will need some background knowledge about the nature and typical magnitude of the temperature coefficient of resistance of metals. Your physics text book will give you information on this. You will also need some knowledge of capacitors. If you have not yet covered capacitors in your theory lessons your teacher can give you the small amount of information about them which you need.

The test involves plotting and comparing a straight line graph with a roughly exponential curve. For help in drawing the curve refer to the hints on page 32. The curve has to be extrapolated back to obtain an extra result. You will not find this an accurate procedure.

Test 8

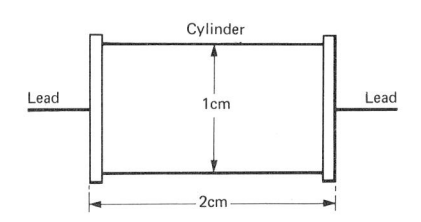

Fig. 4.8 The unknown component.

A student came across the unmarked electronic component shown in Fig. 4.8 on a laboratory bench and decided to do some electrical tests to identify it.

From its appearance and size he thought that it might be either a capacitor or some form of resistor. He measured its resistance at room temperature with an AVO meter and found it to be 500 Ω. He thereupon rejected the idea that it might be a capacitor.

As a further aid to identification he tested how the resistance varied with temperature by connecting the component to a commercial form of Wheatstone bridge and immersing it in a heated water bath. At the same time for comparison he measured the resistance of a copper coil immersed in the same bath. The results shown in Table 4.8 were obtained. The student plotted resistance against temperature for the unknown component and the coil and came to the conclusion that the unknown was not a metal resistance coil.

Plot the resistance—temperature graph for each component and then answer the following questions:

(1) Why did the student reject the idea that the component might be a capacitor after the first test?

(2) List the three factors shown on your graphs from which you conclude that the unknown is not a metal.

(3) The temperature coefficient of resistance α can be defined as,

$$\alpha = \frac{R_t - R_0}{R_0 t} = \frac{\text{Slope}}{R_0}$$

where R_t is the resistance at $t\,°C$ and R_0 is the resistance at $0\,°C$. Use your graph to find α for the copper coil.

(4) If such a definition of α was applied to the unknown component would it have any validity? Would α be constant?

Resistance of unknown component (Ω)	Resistance of copper coil (Ω)	Temperature (°C)
455·0	5·10	20
331·0	5·15	25
268·0	5·25	30
217·0	5·35	35
181·0	5·42	40
152·0	5·50	45
130·0	5·60	50
109·0	5·70	55
92·0	5·75	60
80·0	5·85	65
70·5	5·92	70
59·0	5·98	75
52·8	6·08	80
45·0	6·18	85
40·0	6·35	90

Table 4.8.

(5) An approximate value for room temperature can be obtained from one of your graphs. What is this value and why is it only approximate?

(6) Give one reason why the copper coil graph appears to have a much greater scatter on it than the unknown component graph.

Conclusion

The unknown device was in fact a thermistor. Thermistors are made from a mixture of metal oxides and have semi-conductor properties, in particular a large and negative temperature coefficient of resistance.

Small thermistors are used for temperature measurement and control, but the large one described above would not respond quickly enough to changes in temperature for such purposes. It would be used for the suppression of voltage surges in power supply circuits which feed electronic equipment.

Test Nine

An experiment with an iron–copper thermocouple

Test 9

This test involves plotting a parabola and measuring its maximum. You will also have to measure its slope at various points and use the values obtained to plot a straight line graph as required by question 3. Since the curve is fairly shallow you will probably find it easiest to draw the tangents by the first method described on page 34. Question 4 requires you to draw another straight line graph and the comparison between this and the previous straight line graph is best observed if both are drawn on the same set of axes.

In 1821 Seebeck discovered that if the junctions of two different metals in a circuit are maintained at different temperatures an e.m.f. is developed. The phenomenon is called the thermoelectric or Seebeck effect and the arrangement is called a thermocouple.

The e.m.f. of a thermocouple, generally of the order of millivolts, may be measured using a potentiometer and a simple circuit is shown in Fig. 4.9(a). Complete details of the measurement can be found in your physics text book.

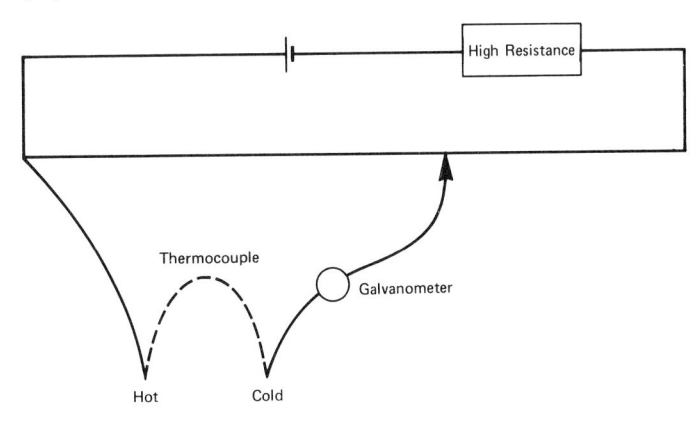

Fig. 4.9(a) Measuring thermo-electric e.m.f.

Temperature of cold junction = 0°C.

Temperature of the hot junction t, °C	Thermo-electric e.m.f. E, (mV)
20	1·70
40	3·24
60	4·62
80	5·84
100	6·90
120	7·80
140	8·54
160	9·04
180	9·45
200	9·16
220	9·68
240	9·60
260	9·36
280	8·96

Table 4.9.

If one junction (the cold junction) of a thermocouple is maintained at 0°C and the temperature of the other junction (the hot junction) is altered the variation of the thermoelectric e.m.f. with the temperature of the hot junction is as shown in Fig. 4.9(b).

The curve is a parabola and has the equation,

$$E = at + bt^2$$

where E is the thermoelectric e.m.f., t is the temperature difference in degrees Celsius between the two junctions (since the cold junction is at 0°C t is also the temperature of the hot junction) and a and b are constants which depend upon the two metals used.

Fig. 4.9(b) Thermo-electric e.m.f. variation with temperature.

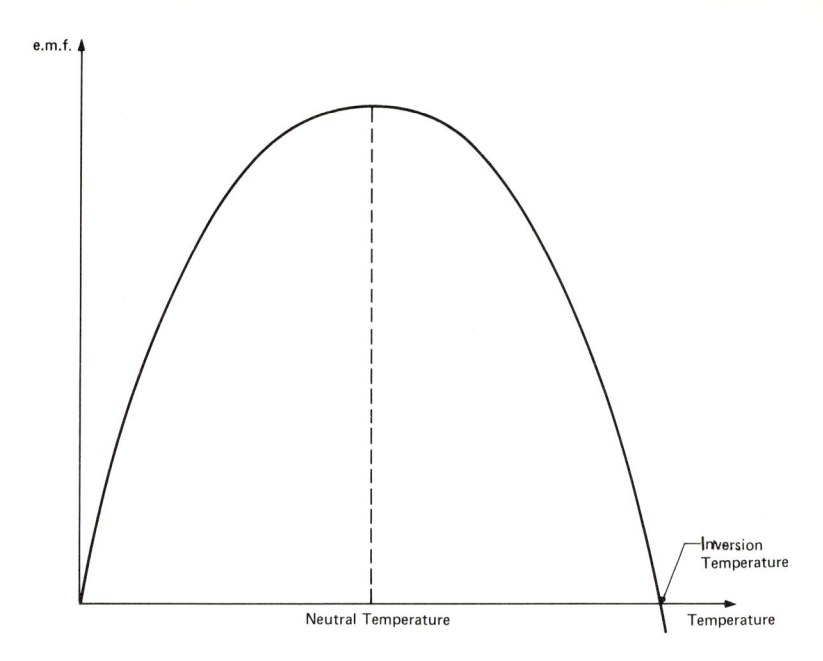

The results of an experiment with an iron–copper thermocouple are given in Table 4.9. The temperature of the cold junction was maintained at 0°C throughout so that the results fit the equation $E = at + bt^2$. Using these results plot a graph of E against t and answer the following questions:

(1) From your graph find the neutral temperature (temperature at which the e.m.f. is a maximum) and comment on the accuracy of its value.

(2) If the cold junction had been maintained at 50°C throughout the experiment what would the e.m.f. be when the hot junction is at 90°C?

(3) If the equation $E = at + bt^2$ is differentiated with respect to temperature difference we obtain,

$$\frac{dE}{dt} = a + 2bt$$

where dE/dt is the thermoelectric power, that is, the slope of the E against t graph.

At various points on your E against t graph, draw tangents to find dE/dt. Plot dE/dt against t and from your graph obtain values for a and b. You may find some scatter of your points. Why do you think this is so?

(4) Examine the equation $E = at + bt^2$ carefully. It is possible to rearrange this equation in the form $y = mx + c$ to obtain a straight line. Obtain this form of the equation, draw the required graph and find the values of a and b. Compare these values with those obtained in question 3. Which values for a and b do you consider to be most reliable? Give reasons.

(5) Would the particular combination of iron and copper make a practical thermocouple for measuring temperatures in the range 200°C to 400°C?

Test Ten

The moment of inertia of a solid cylinder

Test 10

This test uses the results of a standard laboratory experiment to find the moment of inertia of a solid cylinder. Using the theory, and the results obtained, you have to choose suitable quantities to plot so that the moment of inertia can be calculated from the slope of the graph.

A rolling object has kinetic energy of both translation and rotation so that its total energy is given by,

total energy = translational kinetic energy + rotational kinetic energy

$$= \tfrac{1}{2}mv^2 + \tfrac{1}{2}I\omega^2$$

where m is the mass of the object, I its moment of inertia about the axis concerned, v its translational velocity and ω its angular velocity.

Clearly the moment of inertia must be known if the total energy of the object is to be found. If an object has symmetry then its moment of inertia is easy to measure and an experiment is described in this test to find the moment of inertia of a solid cylinder about an axis through its centre and perpendicular to its end faces.

The cylinder was rolled from rest down an inclined plane and the time to travel a distance AB was measured. The experiment was repeated for different values of the vertical height h of the starting point A above the line BC and the corresponding times to roll the distance AB were measured. (See Fig. 4.10). The results given in Table 4.10 were obtained.

If m is the mass of the cylinder of radius a and I is the moment of inertia about the axis concerned then equating,

potential energy lost = kinetic energy of translation + kinetic energy of rotation

we obtain

$$mgh = \tfrac{1}{2}mv^2 + \tfrac{1}{2}I\omega^2$$

where v is the final translational velocity, ω is the final angular velocity and g is the acceleration due to gravity. Using $v = a\omega$ we have,

$$mgh = \frac{1}{2}mv^2 + \frac{1}{2}I\frac{v^2}{a^2}$$

v is twice the average velocity as the acceleration is uniform and hence

$$v = \frac{2s}{t}$$

where s is the distance AB and t is the time to roll the distance AB from rest.

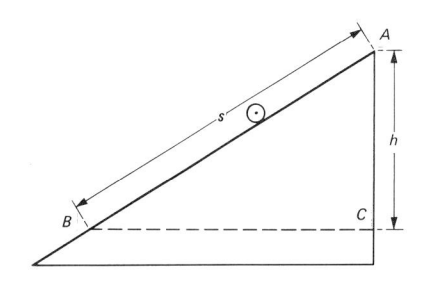

Fig. 4.10 Moment of inertia of a cylinder.

Distance AB = 2·0 m
Mass of cylinder = 2·5 kg
Radius of cylinder = 15 mm

Vertical fall h, (m)	Time to roll distance AB from rest t, (s)
0·05	5·00
0·10	3·43
0·15	2·89
0·20	2·46
0·25	2·21
0·30	2·02
0·35	1·87
0·40	1·75
0·45	1·64
0·50	1·54

Table 4.10.

Therefore $$mgh = \frac{1}{2}m\left(\frac{2s}{t}\right)^2 + \frac{1}{2}\frac{I}{a^2}\left(\frac{2s}{t}\right)^2$$

Therefore $$2gh = \left(\frac{2s}{t}\right)^2 + \frac{I}{ma^2}\left(\frac{2s}{t}\right)^2$$

Using the results in Table 4.10 plot a graph so that the moment of inertia of the cylinder may be obtained from the slope of the graph. (Assume $g = 9 \cdot 8$ ms^{-2}). Answer the following questions:

(1) What would be the effect on the time t if the plane was smooth enough for the cylinder to slide rather than roll?

(2) What causes a body to roll rather than slide down an inclined plane?

(3) If a photograph had been taken of the cylinder rolling down the slope the lower part may be distinct whilst the upper part is blurred. Explain why this is so.

Test Eleven

Experiments to investigate Newton's law of cooling

Test 11

The first part of this test involves the plotting of a cooling curve and then drawing tangents to the curve to decide whether Newton's law of cooling is obeyed for a body cooling under conditions of forced convection. The same procedure is then used to see if there is a relationship between draught speed and rate of cooling.

Newton's law of cooling states that in conditions of forced convection (that is, a draught) the rate of loss of heat from a body is directly proportional to the excess temperature over the surroundings. That is,

$$\frac{dQ}{dt} = k(\theta - \theta_0)$$

where dQ/dt is the rate of loss of heat at the temperature θ and θ_0 is the surrounding temperature. k is a constant for a given body under given conditions, its value depending mainly on the area and the nature of the surface and the nature and pressure of the surrounding gas.

Since
$$\frac{dQ}{dt} = mc\frac{d\theta}{dt}$$

then
$$\frac{d\theta}{dt} = \frac{k}{mc}(\theta - \theta_0)$$

where m is the mass of the body, c its specific heat capacity and $d\theta/dt$ the rate of cooling. Therefore,

$$\frac{d\theta}{dt} = K(\theta - \theta_0)$$

where
$$K = \frac{k}{mc}$$

(Strictly speaking to be mathematically correct the equation should be written

$$\frac{d\theta}{dt} = -K(\theta - \theta_0)$$

since $d\theta/dt$ is a rate of cooling).

The results in Table 4.11(a) were taken by a student for a heated polished cylinder cooling under conditions of forced convection (constant draught speed). He measured the values of the excess temperature of the body over the surroundings $(\theta - \theta_0)$ at regular intervals.

Using the student's results plot a cooling curve of excess temperature

Excess temperature (°C)	Time (s)
316	0
238	40
178	80
135	120
102	160
77	200
58	240
44	280

Table 4.11(a).

against time. Draw tangents to your cooling curve at several points and evaluate the rate of cooling. Plot the rate of cooling against the corresponding excess temperature and if Newton's law of cooling is obeyed a straight line graph passing through the origin will be obtained. Obtain the slope K from the graph. Answer the following questions:

(1) Does your graph verify Newton's law of cooling? Your graph may show a scatter of points. Why do you think this is so?
(2) If the surface of the cylinder had been blackened explain how the slope K of the graph would have changed. Give reasons for this.

The student knew that Newton's law of cooling only applies for excess temperatures of 30°C or more and in conditions of forced convection. He wanted to see what relationship, if any, exists between draught speed and rate of cooling. He produced a series of cooling curves for different draught speeds and his results are shown in Table 4.11(b).

Draught speed (ms^{-1})	Excess temperatures taken at intervals of 40 s (°C)						
4·6	184	162	143	126	111	97	85
5·8	163	139	119	103	88	75	64
6·4	184	160	139	120	103	89	76
8·9	144	121	101	83	68	55	44
11·0	156	127	104	85	68	54	42

Table 4.11(b).

Plot the cooling curve for each draught speed and for a given excess temperature (for example 110°C) try to establish a relationship between the draught speed and the rate of cooling. *Hint*—present the results graphically.

Test Twelve

Background radiation in the laboratory

Test 12

This test involves one of the very few situations where a dot to dot plotted graph is required; the reason being that the problem involves a random process. This has already been mentioned on pages 29 and 31.

In all radioactivity experiments in the laboratory we come up against the problem of the measurement of background radiation. This is the number of counts registered by the detector (Geiger Muller tube and scaler) due to cosmic rays, distant sources in the laboratory, luminous watches, radioactivity of the soil and so on. We need to measure the background count rate in order to obtain a value for the true count rate when a radioactive source is placed near the detector. The problem arises—how many counts or for how long do we need to count to get an accurate value for the background count rate? This is not as simple as it sounds since radioactive decay is a random process and obeys certain statistical laws which we must use correctly to obtain an accurate count rate.

The following theory applies to any random process but we will apply it specifically to radioactive processes. Suppose in a period of time t our scaler registers N counts (either due to background or to a source in front of the Geiger Muller tube).

If we repeat the measurement several times we will get a fairly wide variation in N. Since the radioactive decay processes are random, statistical laws predict that the probable error involved in measuring N counts is $\sqrt{N}$. That is the number of counts $= N \pm \sqrt{N}$ and the greater the number of counts the greater the probable error becomes. However the percentage error is given by

$$\frac{\sqrt{N}}{N} \times 100 = \frac{100}{\sqrt{N}}$$

so that as the number of counts taken increases the probable percentage error falls. This is the form of probable error that we normally use.

It is clear that the percentage accuracy of the count (and count rate also) depends on the total number of counts N taken irrespective of the time involved. Using percentage error $= 100/\sqrt{N}$

for 10% accuracy $\dfrac{100}{\sqrt{N}} = 10$ therefore $N = 100$ counts

for 5% accuracy $\dfrac{100}{\sqrt{N}} = 5$ therefore $N = 400$ counts

for 1% accuracy $\dfrac{100}{\sqrt{N}} = 1$ therefore $N = 10000$ counts

and so on.

If we were using a radioactive source giving say 2000 counts per minute then we could attain a one per cent accuracy in a time of five minutes.

If we were counting background radiation of approximately 20 counts per minute we would need a count time of five hundred minutes to attain the same accuracy. This is clearly not practical since the background count may change in this time due to air circulation changes, people entering and leaving the laboratory, etc.

To try out some of these ideas and observe the fluctuations in the background in a busy laboratory a student set a Geiger Muller tube on the bench totally exposed and connected to a scaler. He observed the accumulated count at various time intervals as shown in Table 4.12.

Elapsed time minutes	Total counts	Count rate based on sequential one minute intervals	Cumulative count rate (counts/min)
0	0	0	0
0·25	4		16·0
0·50	6		12·0
0·75	7		9·0
1·0	17	17	17·0
1·5	17		11·3
2·0	21	4	10·5
3·0	32	11	10·7
4·0	48	16	12·0
5·0	55	7	11·0
6·0	65		
7·0	81		
8·0	90		
9·0	97		
10·0	115		
11·0	138		
12·0	149		
13·0	166		
14·0	182		
15·0	192		
16·0	206		
17·0	216		
18·0	228		
19·0	232		
20·0	246		
21·0	254		
22·0	264		
23·0	283		
24·0	297		
25·0	312		

Table 4.12.

There are two ways of treating these results. Either (a) find a count rate for each one minute interval or (b) find a cumulative count rate by dividing the total counts by the total elapsed time. Some of the results have been evaluated to illustrate this. Complete the table and then on the same graph plot the sequential rate and cumulative rate against time. This is one of the rare cases where you must draw straight lines between the points on a graph. The reason is that in this case we are dealing with random processes and hence have no information about probable values between the measured points. Answer the following questions:

(1) Account for the wild and continuous fluctuations in the sequential count rate. What is the range of its probable percentage accuracy?

(2) The cumulative count rate settles to a steady value after 20 minutes. What background count per minute does it indicate and what is the probable accuracy? What is the probable accuracy after 5, 10, 15 minutes?

(3) At what time during the experimental run did extra students (at least one wearing a luminous watch) enter the laboratory?

(4) In a β-ray measurement experiment done in the same laboratory the lowest count rate measured was 30 counts per minute over a two minute interval. What time interval would be used in the background counting at the end of the experiment to obtain similar accuracy?

Test Thirteen

The absorption of β-rays by matter

Test 13

This test is a follow on from Test Twelve in that the ideas concerning background count rate are used in a simple counting experiment. You are asked to plot a log-linear graph of count rate against mass per unit area of an absorber of β-rays (guidance on log-linear graphs is given on pages 22 and 24) and comment on its shape in view of your knowledge of background radiation.

An experimenter attempted to test the laws governing the absorption of β-rays (electrons produced by radioactive nuclear disintegrations) in the following simple way. He had available a Geiger Muller tube, scaler and power supply, a low activity source, a lead castle and a variety of absorbers. He set up the equipment as shown in Fig. 4.13 and measured the count rate for a variety of thicknesses of various absorbers, using a two minute counting interval in every case. His results are shown in Table 4.13. The actual thicknesses of absorber are not quoted directly but mass per unit cross section is used instead. It is easy to understand that

$$\text{density} \times \text{thickness} = \frac{\text{mass}}{\text{unit area}}$$

so that by using mass per unit area instead of thickness we are involving the nature (density) of the absorber as well as its thickness.

The β absorption law is thought to have the form,

$$R = R_0 e^{-c\rho x}$$

where the count rate R is the number of β-rays per second penetrating the thickness x. R_0 is the count rate for zero thickness, ρ the absorber density and c a constant. Clearly ρx = the mass per unit cross section as previously explained. Taking logs we obtain,

$$\log_e R = \log_e R_0 - c\rho x$$

or

$$\log_{10} R = \log_{10} R_0 - c\rho x/2 \cdot 3$$

Hence by plotting $\log_{10} R$ against ρx the form of the equation can be tested. Plot this graph using the results given for aluminium. (Note that because of the cramping effects of a log scale it is not necessary to plot all the results for the thinner absorbers. Make a reasonable selection.) Answer the following questions:

(1) Does your graph verify the form of the above equation? Briefly explain your answer.

(2) Below a count rate of roughly 20 per minute the count rate appears to be independent of ρx for the absorber used. Can you explain this

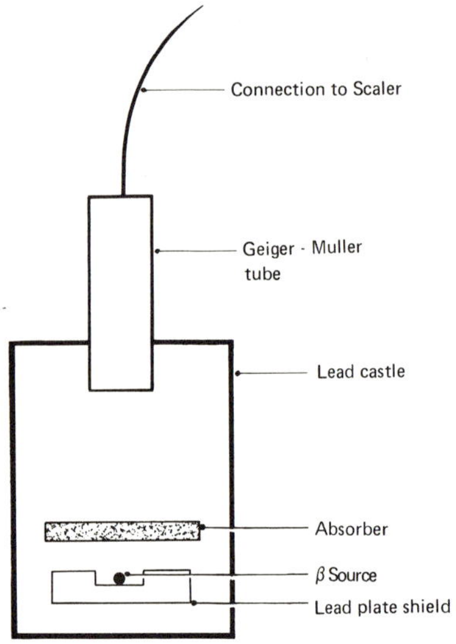

Fig. 4.13 Absorption of β-rays.

Absorber material	Mass/unit area, (mg/cm²)	Counts	Count time (min)	Count rate R (counts/min)	Log₁₀ rate
Aluminium	0	3616	2	1808	3·257
Aluminium	15·5	3440	2	1720	3·235
Aluminium	30·7	2852	2	1426	3·154
Aluminium	52·4	2630	2	1315	3·119
Aluminium	76·2	2492	2	1246	3·095
Aluminium	90·4	2207	2	1103	3·043
Aluminium	125·0	1991	2	996	2·983
Aluminium	182·6	1552	2	776	2·890
Aluminium	248·0	1075	2	537	2·730
Aluminium	332·0	620	2	310	2·491
Aluminium	426·0	314	2	157	2·196
Aluminium	551·0	162	2	81	1·909
Aluminium	631·0	95	2	47	1·672
Aluminium	708·0	60	2	30	1·477
Aluminium	833·0	34	2	17	1·231
Aluminium	920·5	44	2	22	1·343
Aluminium	1000·0	32	2	16	1·204
Lead	1330·0	44	2	22	1·343
Cardboard	88·9	1995	2	997	2·998
Cardboard	264·6	696	2	348	2·542
Glass	310·9	784	2	392	2·593
Perspex	209·0	1019	2	509	2·707

Table 4.13.

effect? Do you think you would still get this count rate if the β source was totally removed from the counter?

(3) Plot the other results obtained on the same graph. Do they fit the line for aluminium? What conclusions can you draw from this?

(4) Find from the graph the following—

(a) the thickness of glass needed to reduce the count rate to 100 per minute (density of glass = 2·90 g cm⁻³).

(b) the thickness of lead needed to reduce the count rate to 100 per minute (density of lead = 11·34 g cm⁻³).

(c) the thickness of aluminium needed to halve the zero thickness count rate. (Density of aluminium = 2·70 g cm⁻³).

(d) what would be the thickness of air needed to halve the zero thickness count rate? (Density of air = 1·29 × 10⁻³ g cm⁻³).

(5) What improvements to the experiment can you suggest to obtain a more accurate slope for the graph?

(6) What would be the effects on the graph of using a source of the same activity but higher energy emission? (β's emitted at the same rate but having higher average energies).

General conclusions and a safety warning

From the work above we can conclude that the β's from the source used in the experiment were easily stopped by quite small thicknesses of moderately dense material. This is true for the β's from most sources used in school and college experiments but it does not apply to γ rays. These are generally ten to one hundred times more penetrating than β-rays of the same energy. The sources used in school experiments are often mixed β–γ emitters and even though they are of low activity and usually shielded no unnecessary exposure should be allowed. Never handle them with bare fingers. Use tongs and do not expose yourself to their radiation for any length of time.

Finally answer the following question:

(7) When storing a high activity, high energy γ source, behind which would you feel safest, 1·0 m of concrete or 0·1 m of lead? (Density of concrete = 2·20 g cm^{-3}). Explain your answer.

Test Fourteen

This test is slightly different from the previous ones that you have done. The experiment described is an attempt to reproduce the results of a very famous experiment carried out by the Italian scientist Galileo. The test involves a rather simple plot of the set of results and gives Galileo's theory and reasoning behind the experiment. When you have plotted the straight line graph and measured its slope you will find that the answer is not what Galileo expected. You are asked to find the flaw in Galileo's theory and to see if you can obtain the correct theory for the experiment.

Test 14

Galileo (1564–1642) showed, with the aid of a water clock, that the distance rolled from rest by a smooth bronze ball down an inclined plane in time t was directly proportional to t^2.

Galileo attempted to see if the above relationship was true for a freely falling body. He realised the difficulty of timing a freely falling body through various heights and approached the problem indirectly by using the inclined plane. Using steeper inclines he was able to show that the distance rolled was always proportional to the square of the time taken, and argued that the relation would hold for the limiting case of a vertical incline. He measured the distance the ball rolled from rest in a given time down planes of various inclinations and extrapolated his results to obtain the distance rolled down a vertical plane. This he equated to the distance the ball would travel from rest in free fall in the given time.

In Fig. 4.14 the chord BA of the circle represents the distance travelled from rest in one second by a ball rolling down a slope inclined at an angle α with the horizontal. It can be shown that other chords of the circle AB_1 and AB_2 represent the distance travelled from rest in one second by the ball rolling down slopes of greater inclinations α_1 and α_2 with the horizontal.

In an attempt to repeat Galileo's experiment the result shown in Table 4.14 were obtained. BA is the distance travelled from rest in the first second and h is the distance of the starting point above the horizontal line AD. Geometry shows that,

$$AB^2 = h \cdot CA$$

Using the above results plot a graph enabling CA to be calculated as the slope. Galileo extrapolated the results obtained by rolling and expected CA to represent the distance fallen vertically from rest in the first second of motion. Knowing CA he could calculate the acceleration due to gravity g.

BA, (m)	h, (m)
0.59	0.1
1.03	0.3
1.32	0.5
1.58	0.7
1.78	0.9
1.96	1.1
2.13	1.3

Table 4.14.

Fig. 4.14 Galileo's experiment.

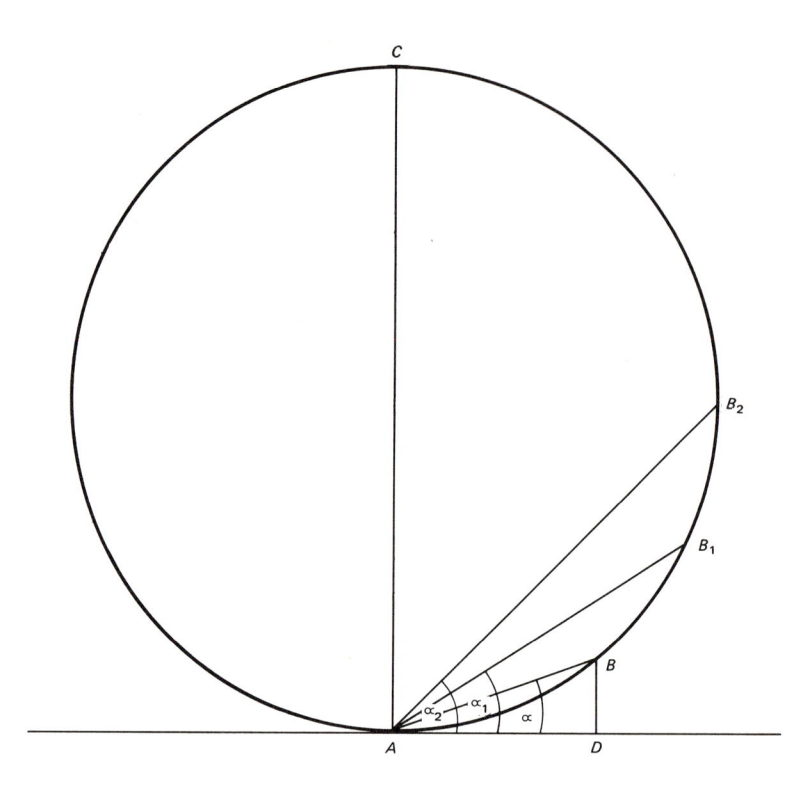

Galileo's reasoning

The potential energy lost by the ball of mass m in falling the distance $CA = mgCA$. The kinetic energy gained by the ball $= \frac{1}{2}mv^2$ where v is the final velocity at A. Therefore,

$$mg.CA = \tfrac{1}{2}mv^2$$

Hence
$$CA = \frac{v^2}{2g}$$

The ball is accelerated uniformly, therefore the average velocity $\bar{v}$ is half the final velocity v. Therefore, $\bar{v} = CA/t$ where t is the time taken to travel the distance CA and is equal to one second. Therefore, $\bar{v} = CA = v/2$ and hence $v = 2CA$. Substituting for v^2 above we obtain $CA = 2CA^2/g$. That is $CA = g/2$. Therefore CA should be equal to 4·9 m.

Answer the following questions:

(1) The value of CA obtained from the slope of your graph is clearly not equal to $g/2$. What is the flaw in Galileo's extrapolation?

(2) Outline the other method of obtaining CA from the graph. (*Hint*—look at Fig. 4.14 again). Which of the two methods do you think would be the most accurate? Give reasons.

(3) Having established the flaw in Galileo's extrapolation modify the above theory to show that CA should be $g/2\cdot8$.

(4) Would it have made any difference to the values of BA if Galileo had used a thin hollow bronze sphere of the same mass and greater radius instead of the solid bronze sphere? Give reasons for your answer.

Test Fifteen

Thermal radiation from a tungsten filament lamp

This test involves the use of a log-log graph to find the form of the dependence of the power dissipated in a filament on the resistance of the filament. You have to compare the results obtained from those predicted by theory and see if you can understand where the theory has made invalid assumptions.

You will find that as so often happens in real experimental situations the form of the dependence is not constant. That is, in the equation $W = KR^n$ neither K nor n are true constants but show a slow variation with R. This is shown by the fact that $\log_{10} W$ against $\log_{10} R$ gives a shallow curve rather than a straight line. To find K and n at a specific power you will have to draw a tangent to the curve.

Test 15

An experiment was carried out using the circuit shown in Fig. 4.15 to test the power which a 12 V, 24 W gas filled headlamp bulb could deliver both above and below 12 V.

Fig. 4.15 The circuit.

Readings for the filament current I and the potential difference V across the filament were taken. These results, which are listed in Table 4.15, were taken in a period of about ten minutes. Calculate the power and the filament resistance for each set of results.

Assuming that the lamp is losing heat only by radiation then the heat lost per second from the surface of the filament $= SAT^4$ where S is a constant, A is the area of the filament and T is the filament temperature measured in degrees absolute.

If the ambient temperature is T_A the heat gained by the filament from the surroundings $= SAT_A^4$.

When equilibrium is reached the power supplied is given by,

$$W = SA(T^4 - T_A^4)$$

which equals the net heat lost per second.

Assuming $T \gg T_A$ then $W = SAT^4$.

If the filament is a pure metal the resistance R can be assumed to be proportional to T. Therefore,

$$\frac{R_A}{R} = \frac{T_A}{T} \quad \text{and} \quad T = T_A \frac{R}{R_A}$$

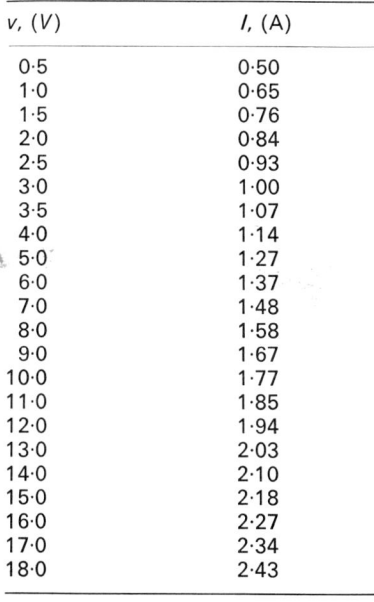

v, (V)	I, (A)
0·5	0·50
1·0	0·65
1·5	0·76
2·0	0·84
2·5	0·93
3·0	1·00
3·5	1·07
4·0	1·14
5·0	1·27
6·0	1·37
7·0	1·48
8·0	1·58
9·0	1·67
10·0	1·77
11·0	1·85
12·0	1·94
13·0	2·03
14·0	2·10
15·0	2·18
16·0	2·27
17·0	2·34
18·0	2·43

Table 4.15.

73

Therefore
$$W = SA\left(\frac{T_A}{R_A}\right)^4 \cdot R^4$$

That is, $W = KR^4$ where $K = SA(T_A/R_A)^4$.

If $\log_{10} W$ is plotted against $\log_{10} R$ a straight line graph should be obtained having a slope of 4 and an intercept of $\log_{10} K$ on the $\log_{10} W$ axis.

Plot the graph of $\log_{10} W$ against $\log_{10} R$. You will find that the graph is a shallow curve and not a straight line and nowhere is the slope equal to 4. Draw tangents to the curve at the normal operating point of 24 W and also at 38 W. Measure the slope of each of these and also the intercept which each makes on the $\log_{10} W$ axis. Write down the true equation of the form $W = KR^n$ at each of these points on the curve using the values of K and n obtained from the tangents. Answer the following questions:

(1) Why does the simple theory above fail to describe the experimental situation? Check the validity of the three assumptions in the theory as far as you can.

(2) Given that $T_A = 300$ K and $R_A = 1\,\Omega$ calculate, using the equations $K = SA(T_A/R_A)^4$ and $W = SAT^4$ the operating temperatures of the filament at 24 W and 38 W. Use the power numbers obtained from your graph and not 4 as in the equations.

(3) The normal running temperature of the filament of a small filament lamp is about 2000 K. How confident are you concerning the value of the temperature which you have obtained for the 38 W dissipation?

(4) The fact that the 12 V, 24 W bulb can be run without failure at 18 V, 44 W may seem surprising. What factors enable the experiment to be carried out under these conditions?

(5) Would you expect to be able to use a 6 V, 45 W headlamp bulb in a car with a 12 V electrical system? If not, state reasons why.

Test Sixteen

The motion of spheres in a viscous medium

This experiment is concerned with the conditions under which Stokes' law for the motion of a sphere through a viscous medium breaks down. You are asked to plot a suitable graph in an attempt to verify the law and then use two forms of a correction formula to replot the graph in an attempt to correct for its departure from a straight line. In order to answer the questions fully you will need to have some knowledge of the viscous behaviour of liquids. Unless you have already covered this in your theory lessons you cannot really tackle the test successfully.

Test 16

An experiment was carried out to see how the terminal velocity of a ball bearing falling freely in a tube of oil was related to its diameter d. The balls were carefully dropped through a small tube into the centre of the main tube which was of diameter 46 mm and the position of marker A (elastic band round tube) was adjusted until it was well below the position at which the ball ceased to accelerate. B was positioned 0·8 m below A and by timing the ball between these marks, its terminal velocity v_t was obtained (see Fig. 4.16(a)). The results shown in Table 4.16(a) were obtained using three balls of each size and taking an average for v_t.

The experimenter thought that at low speeds the probable relationship between v_t and d was,

$$v_t \propto d^2$$

Answer the following questions:

(1) Plot a suitable graph to test the above relationship, but before doing so you must question the validity of the last three results shown in the table. The experimenter was using a stop watch for the timing and had a reaction time of approximately 0·2 s. How accurate do you think his timings would be on the last three balls and are you justified in using such results?

(2) At what terminal velocity does the simple relationship $v_t \propto d^2$ fail? Use your graph to find this.

One of the reasons for the breakdown of the simple relationship is 'wall effect'. When the sphere falls through the oil not only does it force the oil to flow over its own surface but also over the part of the surface of the containing tube nearest the ball. (See Fig. 4.16(b)). This exerts extra viscous drag on the ball so that its terminal velocity is lower than it would be if the ball fell freely in an infinite medium. The simple $v_t \propto d^2$ relationship assumes such a medium. A correction formula for v_t exists. This gives,

$$v_{tm} = v_{tinf}\left[1 - 2\cdot104\frac{d}{D} + 2\cdot09\left(\frac{d}{D}\right)^3 - 0\cdot95\left(\frac{d}{D}\right)^5\right]$$

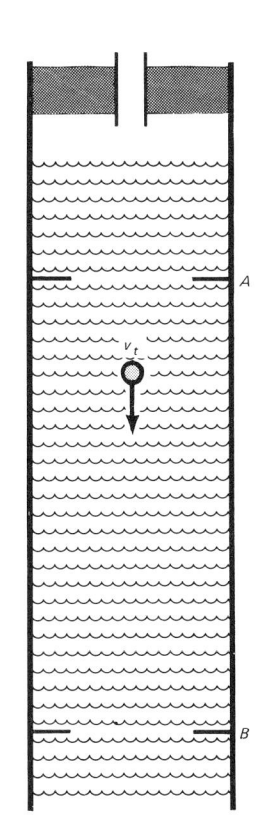

Fig. 4.16(a) The apparatus.

Fig. 4.16(b) The wall effect.

Drag on ball due to motion of liquid over this region of the tube wall.

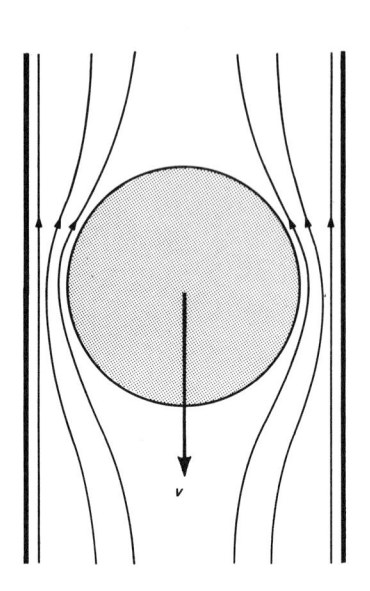

Ball diameter d, (mm)	Terminal velocity v_t, (mm s^{-1})	(Ball diameter)^2 d^2, (mm)^2
1·54	9·5	2·4
2·38	20·8	5·7
3·18	35·0	10·1
3·97	50·3	15·8
4·76	71·0	22·7
6·35	114·3	40·3
9·58	194·5	91·8
12·71	291·0	162·0
15·88	350·0	252·1
19·06	350·0	363·8
25·40	350·0	645·2

Table 4.16(a).

where v_{tm} is the measured terminal velocity, v_{tinf} is the terminal velocity in an infinite medium, d is the ball diameter and D is the tube diameter. Use this formula to obtain corrected values v_{tinf} for the terminal velocity in the following way.

For the first four results where $d \ll D$ fairly accurate corrections can be obtained using,

$$v_{tm} = v_{tinf}\left[1 - 2 \cdot 104 \frac{d}{D}\right]$$

since $(d/D)^3$ is negligible. For the next four results you must use,

$$v_{tm} = v_{tinf}\left[1 - 2 \cdot 104 \frac{d}{D} + 2 \cdot 09 \left(\frac{d}{D}\right)^3\right]$$

since $(d/D)^3$ is no longer negligible. $(d/D)^5$ can be neglected in both cases. Do not use the last three results, as for a variety of reasons, they are unreliable. Tabulate your results as shown in Table 4.16(b) and plot on your existing graph v_{tinf} against d^2. You will have to draw a new v_t scale to do this. (Lay it out in a similar way to the scales in Fig. A.8(a)).

(3) After examination of your new graph do you consider that 'wall effect' fully accounts for the departure from $v_t \propto d^2$ at the higher values of v_t? If not, what other process can you suggest which may become important at the higher velocities and what effect will it have on v_t? Are the results obtained good enough to lead to definite conclusions about any such process?

(4) Given a reasonable choice of equipment such as might be found in your laboratory and using the same oil as before, how would you test the full form of the correction equation,

$$v_{tm} = v_{tinf}\left[1 - 2 \cdot 104 \frac{d}{D} + 2 \cdot 09 \left(\frac{d}{D}\right)^3 - 0 \cdot 95 \left(\frac{d}{D}\right)^5\right]$$

$\begin{bmatrix}\text{Ball}\\\text{diameter}\end{bmatrix}^2$ d^2, (mm)^2	Uncorrected terminal velocity v_{tm}, (mm s^{-1})	$\dfrac{d}{D}$	$\left(\dfrac{d}{D}\right)^3$	$v_{tinf} = \dfrac{v_{tm}}{\left(1 - 2\cdot 104 \dfrac{d}{D}\right)}$	$v_{tinf} = \dfrac{v_{tm}}{\left[1 - 2\cdot 104 \dfrac{d}{D} + 2\cdot 09 \left(\dfrac{d}{D}\right)^3\right]}$
2·4	9·5	3·35 × 10^{-2}	3·75 × 10^{-5}		
5·7	20·8	5·17 × 10^{-2}	1·38 × 10^{-4}		
10·1	35·0	6·91 × 10^{-2}	3·30 × 10^{-4}		
15·8	50·3	8·63 × 10^{-2}	6·43 × 10^{-4}		
22·7	71·0	10·34 × 10^{-2}	11·50 × 10^{-4}		
40·3	114·3	13·80 × 10^{-2}	26·20 × 10^{-4}		
91·8	194·5	20·65 × 10^{-2}	88·50 × 10^{-4}		
162·0	291·0	27·60 × 10^{-2}	208·0 × 10^{-4}		

Table 4.16(b).

keeping the velocities v_{tm} low enough to be measured accurately with a stop watch but using balls such that d/D had a range 0·03 to 0·95?

(5) How would you expect v_{tm} to vary in this second experiment? *Hint*—consider the behaviour of v_{tm} as shown by your first uncorrected graph and then consider what would physically happen as $d \to D$. That is, the ball becomes a fairly tight fit in the tube.

(6) The correction formula is no help in answering Question 5. It only states that $v_{tm} \to v_{tinf} \times 0\cdot 036$ as $d \to D$. Does this mean that v_{tm} is very small and v_{tinf} moderate, or v_{tm} moderate and v_{tinf} huge when $d \to D$? Only by considering what is physically happening when $d \to D$ can this be answered. Does the correction formula hold rigorously when $d = D$?

(7) Of what important mechanical device should you be reminded by the motion of the ball when $d \to D$?

(8) What would be the general effect on the measured terminal velocities of using steel cubes of the same density and mass as the balls actually used? What general conclusions can we draw about the effects of shape on terminal velocity?

Test Seventeen

Experiments with Moiré fringes

Fig. 4.17(a) Moiré pattern produced by a fence and its shadow.

You have no doubt observed the patterns produced by folds in a net curtain or by overlapping reeded blinds. Have you noticed how the pattern changes when there is slight movement of the curtain or blinds? These patterns are called moiré fringes.

Moiré fringes can be seen whenever a structure which repeats itself overlaps another similar structure and the line elements are nearly superposed. For example a picket fence when illuminated by the sun at an angle has shadows which appear to converge due to perspective. The resulting moiré pattern produced by the fence and its shadow consists of curved lines. (See Fig. 4.17(a)). Moiré patterns can also be observed on the television screen due to the interference between patterns in the scene to be transmitted and the characteristic lines across the television screen. People appearing on television are advised not to wear striped clothing because the slightest movement can produce a moiré pattern.

The formation of a moiré pattern can be illustrated using two gratings of equally spaced parallel lines. In Fig. 4.17(b) when the lines overlap at right angles a square grid is seen. However when the lines make an angle of about 45° or less a new set of lines, which are the moiré fringes, appear (see Fig. 4.17(c)). If the angle is reduced still further the moiré fringes become more prominent and the distance between the fringes increases (see Fig. 4.17(d)).

It can be shown that the distance d between the moiré fringes, produced by overlapping two equally spaced gratings, is given by,

$$d = \frac{a}{2 \sin \theta/2}$$

where a is the line spacing of the gratings and θ is the acute angle between the two sets of lines. If θ is small then,

$$d = \frac{a}{\theta}$$

where θ is now in radians. From this equation it follows that, if a and d are known, the moiré technique provides a simple way of determining a small angle θ.

To test the above ideas a student carried out the following experiment. He measured the values of the fringe spacing d at various values of θ for each of two pairs of gratings, one pair having spacing a_1 and the other pair having spacing a_2. A travelling microscope was used to measure d and the rotated grating of each pair was placed flat on the table of a spectrometer and the other held stationary in contact with the first. His results are shown in Table 4.17.

Grating spacings = a_1		Grating spacings = a_2	
d, (mm)	θ, (degrees)	d, (mm)	θ, (degrees)
22·9	1	34·3	1
11·5	2	17·2	2
7·6	3	11·4	3
5·7	4	8·6	4
4·6	5	6·9	5
3·8	6	5·8	6

Table 4.17.

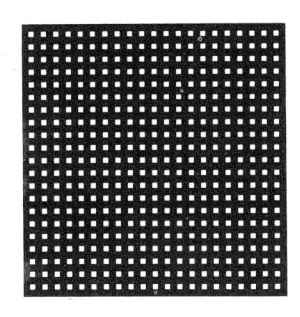

Fig. 4.17(b) Coarse gratings at 90°.

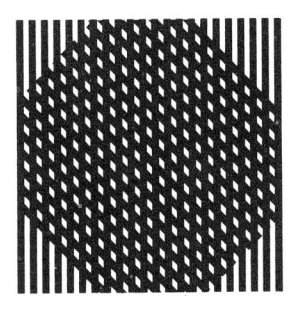

Fig. 4.17(c) Coarse gratings at about 45°.

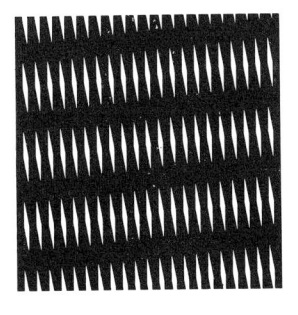

Fig. 4.17(d) Coarse gratings at a small angle.

Using the equation $d = a/\theta$, plot suitable graphs to enable a_1 and a_2 to be calculated. Using the results quoted for the gratings of spacings a_1 plot a calibration curve of d against θ (in degrees) and then answer the following questions:

(1) From the calibration curve of d against θ obtain a value of θ for a fringe spacing of $d = 10$ mm.

(2) Explain why the moiré fringe technique, based on the equation $d = a/\theta$ is unsuitable for measuring very small angles and angles greater than about 10°.

It can be shown that if the line spacings of the two overlapping gratings are not equal then the spacing of the moiré fringes d is given by,

$$d = \frac{a_1 a_2}{\sqrt{(a_1^2 + a_2^2 - 2a_1 a_2 \cos \theta)}}$$

where a_1 and a_2 are the respective spacings of the two line gratings and θ is the acute angle between the two sets of lines.

The student used one grating from each of the previous pairs to make up a pair of gratings of spacings a_1 and a_2 the values of which were known. He then used the above equation to calculate d for various values of θ in the range 0° to 30°. He plotted d against θ but was unable to make accurate measurements of d to confirm the theoretical values.

Using your values of a_1 and a_2 calculate the values of d for θ in the range 0° to 30° and plot d against θ (in degrees). Answer the following questions:

(3) Write down the largest increase in the fringe spacing for an increase in the value of θ of 3°. Hence discuss the suitability of using this pair of unequal gratings for measuring small angular changes, bearing in mind that the accuracy of the travelling microscope used is ± 0.05 mm.

(4) Show that if $a_1 = a_2 = a$ then the equation

$$d = \frac{a_1 a_2}{\sqrt{(a_1^2 + a_2^2 - 2a_1 a_2 \cos \theta)}} \quad \text{becomes} \quad d = \frac{a}{2 \sin \theta/2}$$

(5) If, in the original experiment with a pair of equally spaced gratings, the upper fixed grating has been raised a few millimetres, would the fringes observed be the same as those produced by a pair of unequal gratings in contact? Give reasons for your answer.

Test Eighteen

The design and use of a sunshine recorder

Many seaside towns run small weather recording stations, the most important feature of which is a sunshine recorder. This is frequently mounted on a tall building so that it has an uninterrupted view of the sky. It may well also be above mist level and there are occasional allegations of unfair practice between rival resorts concerning the positioning of the recorder.

The form of recorder normally used is the Campbell–Stokes type. This comprises a glass sphere with a card recording element mounted at its focal surface. The sphere focuses the sun's rays from any direction onto the card and when the intensity of radiation exceeds 15 mW cm^{-2} a burn is produced. The device only gives a sun/no sun record but has the advantage of having no moving parts. It cannot record the intensity variations during the day.

An OND student at a seaside technical college decided as a course project, in the summer term, to try to build a differential sunshine recorder, that is, one which would record and measure direct solar radiation but would ignore 'sky' radiation scattered by the air molecules, water droplets in clouds, etc. He was influenced in his choice of project by the fact that a partial solar eclipse was due at the end of term and this he hoped to measure.

With help from his lecturers he worked out the following theory based on Stefan's radiation law.

Consider a small blackened sphere in a transparent enclosure whose walls are at an absolute temperature T_B. (See Fig. 4.18(a)).

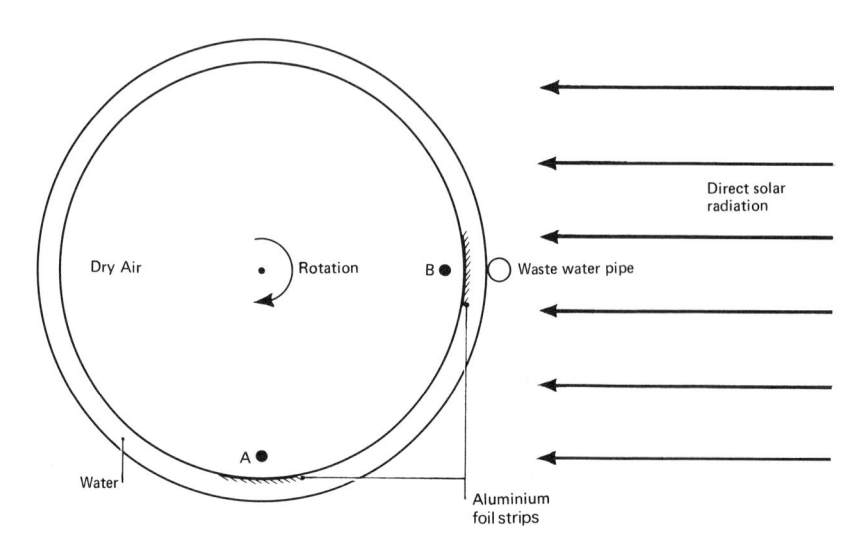

Fig. 4.18(a) A small blackened sphere in a transparent enclosure.

The sphere reaches thermal equilibrium at an absolute temperature of T_1 when its re-radiation rate balances the radiation per second falling on it. That is,

$$4\pi r^2 \sigma T_1^4 = 4\pi r^2 \sigma T_B^4 + 4\pi r^2 D + \pi r^2 I$$

r = sphere radius
D = sky radiation (in W m^{-2}) averaged over 4π steradians
I = direct solar radiation (in W m^{-2})
σ = Stefan's constant.

The equation ignores any conduction or convection losses from the small sphere.

If the sphere were shielded from the direct solar radiation then the equation would be,

$$4\pi r^2 \sigma T_2^4 = 4\pi r^2 \sigma T_B^4 + 4\pi r^2 D$$

That is, the sphere would have an equilibrium temperature (absolute) of T_2 which is less than T_1.

These equations can be rearranged into,

$$T_1^4 - T_B^4 = \frac{D}{\sigma} + \frac{I}{4\sigma}$$

and

$$T_2^4 - T_B^4 = \frac{D}{\sigma}$$

A rough calculation showed that using the minimum value of I detectable (150 W m^{-2}) on the conventional recorder T_1 was only 5°C or 6°C greater than T_B and T_2 even closer. Hence the approximation,

$$T_1^4 - T_B^4 = (T_1^2 - T_B^2)(T_1^2 + T_B^2)$$
$$= (T_1 - T_B)(T_1 + T_B)(T_1^2 + T_B^2)$$
$$= (T_1 - T_B)4T_B^3 \text{ (Taking } T_1 \simeq T_B \text{ here)}$$

could be used. Similarly,

$$T_2^4 - T_B^4 = (T_2 - T_B)4T_B^3$$

This gives
$$(T_1 - T_B)4T_B^3 = \frac{D}{\sigma} + \frac{I}{4\sigma}$$

and
$$(T_2 - T_B)4T_B^3 = \frac{D}{\sigma}$$

Subtracting we obtain $$(T_1 - T_2) = \frac{I}{16\sigma T_B^3}$$

which is a differential result between a shaded and an unshaded sphere.

This gave the student the idea of using a thermocouple as the sensing element, the hot junction to be imbedded in a small sphere fully exposed and the cold junction in a sphere shaded from direct solar radiation. Since the output of a thermocouple is dependent on the temperature difference of the junctions the output (fed to a millivoltmeter) would be a direct measurement of I and by recording this output the variation of I through the day could be obtained.

Fig. 4.18(b) Plan view of recorder.

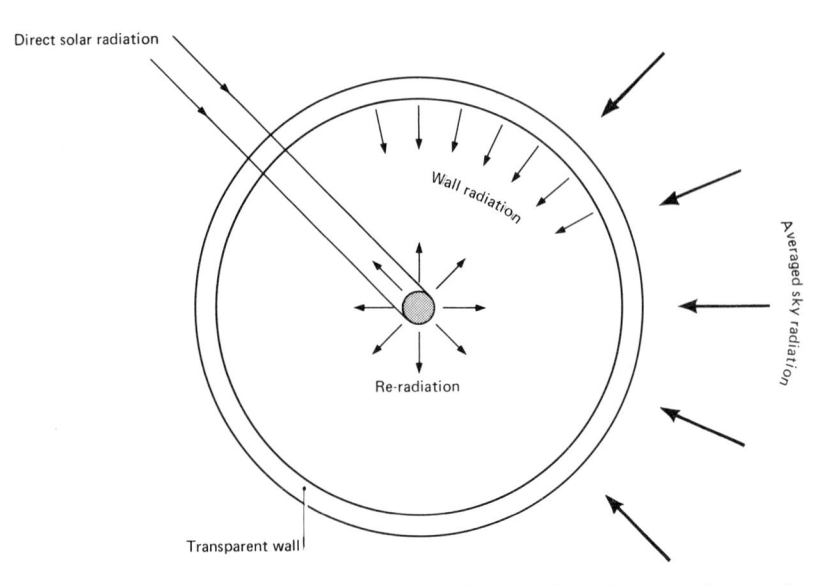

The design problem was to mount the two junctions so that each had the same view of the sky but one was shielded from the direct solar radiation at any position of the sun. Also T_B had to be kept constant. A clockwork driven telescope mount was available in the college science department and the student decided that by mounting his rig on this the shaded junction could be made to follow the sun

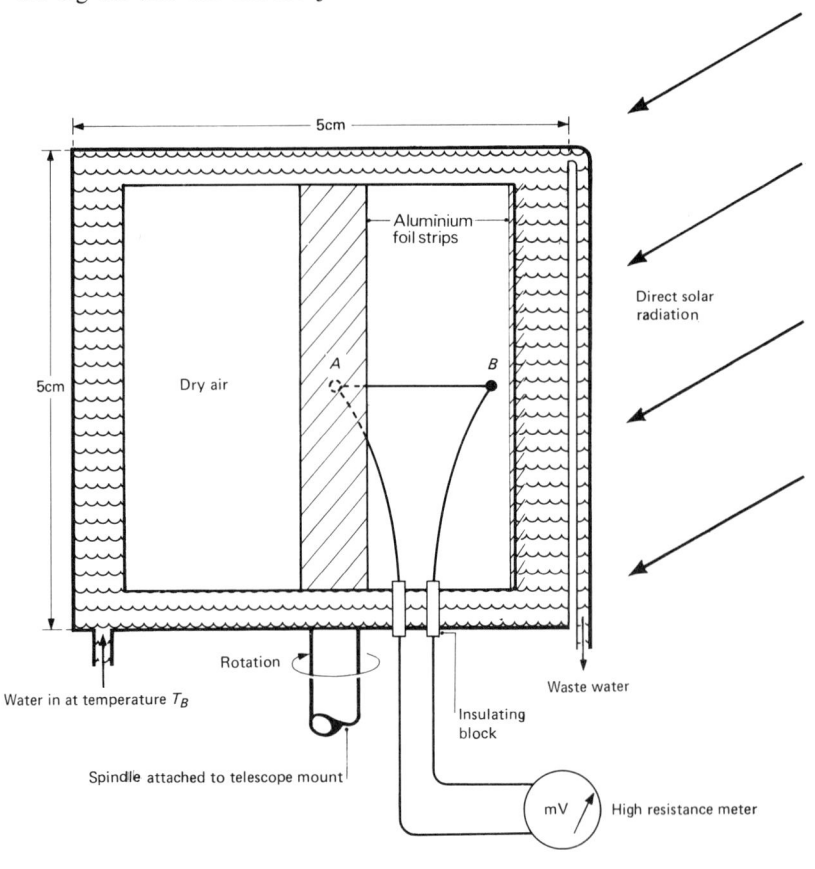

Fig. 4.18(c) Side view of recorder.

satisfactorily. To maintain T_B constant he decided to use a hollow water cooled perspex cylinder to enclose the junctions (mains water temperature is fairly constant at 14°C). He made up the rig shown in Figs. 4.18(b and c). A is the totally exposed junction sphere and B is shaded at all times by its foil strip as the rig rotates to follow the sun. The couple materials used were copper and constantan since these give a fairly large output for a given temperature difference. By using fairly thick wires the junctions were made self supporting although the student realised that this would mean appreciable conduction losses down the leads. The spheres were simply balls of black plasticine of 2 mm diameter.

Questions on the above design

(1) Do junctions A and B have exactly the same view of the sky (apart from the direct solar radiation)? What is the function of the foil strip nearest to A? What is the function of the strip in front of B and why does the water waste pipe run down in front of it?

(2) Why is it desirable to have the millivoltmeter some distance away from the apparatus?

(3) Why should the spheres be small (2 mm diameter)? What are the objections to spheres of say 2 cm diameter?

(4) The student's theory made a major assumption that energy is only lost from the spheres by radiation. Discuss briefly how far the assumption is valid. What effects would you expect any invalidity to have on the temperatures T_1 and T_2 and would their difference be affected?

Calibration and use of the transducer

The student set the transducer up on a high flat roof with a clear view of the sky, running the leads (screened from direct sunlight) into the room below where they were connected to a high impedance (transistorised) millivoltmeter. The use of such a meter avoided the necessity of calibrating the thermocouple and meter together since the impedance was so high that the meter drew virtually no current from the thermocouple. The e.m.f.—temperature difference relationship obtained from tables could be used. He aligned B with the sun at the beginning of a fine morning and started the motor. He took readings at approximately one hour intervals (a few extra near mid-day) throughout the day varying the times of reading slightly to avoid the effects of clouds. The results obtained are shown in Table 4.18(a). The e.m.f.–temperature difference obtained from tables for copper–constantan is shown in Table 4.18(b). Plot this calibration gaph and use it to convert the e.m.f. values in Table 4.18(a) into values of $(T_1 - T_2)$ and finally using

$$(T_1 - T_2) = \frac{I}{16\sigma T_B^3}$$

(taking $\sigma = 5 \cdot 7 \times 10^{-8}$ W m^{-2} K^{-4}, $T_B = 287$ K) convert $(T_1 - T_2)$ values into values of I. Plot the variation of I throughout the day and answer the following questions about it.

(5) The solar constant S is the energy per second per unit area normal to the sun's rays falling on the earth from the sun. It has a value of 1387 W m^{-2}.

Local time (hrs)	mV meter reading (mV)
9·00	0·89
10·03	0·90
11·00	0·90
11·34	0·89
12·02	0·88
12·31	0·88
13·00	0·85
13·28	0·82
14·05	0·76
15·01	0·70
16·04	0·64
17·01	0·59
18·00	0·52
19·00	0·36
20·00	0·18

Table 4.18(a).

Temperature difference, (°C)	E.M.F. (mV)
0	0
10	0.39
20	0.79
30	1.19
40	1.61
50	2.03

Table 4.18(b).

Local time (hrs)	Calculated value of I (Wm^{-2})
9.00	480
10.00	487
11.00	489
11.30	485
11.45	480
12.00	400
12.15	335
12.30	332
12.45	326
13.00	329
13.15	330
13.30	336
13.45	373
14.00	416
15.00	379
16.00	350
17.00	323
18.00	282

Table 4.18(c).

(a) Why do none of the values of I on the graph approach the value of S?

(b) Why does I appear to vary throughout the day?

(c) Calculate the absorption factor of the atmosphere at 12.00 hours on the day the results were taken.

(6) What total energy did sphere A receive due to direct solar radiation between 9.00 hours and 18.00 hours? (*Hint*—for the method of doing this see page 25).

(7) Give one possible reason why the graph is not symmetrical about 12.00 hours local time.

The student decided that he could not spend the time taking results manually throughout the day so he connected his thermocouple to a d.c. amplifier and pen recorder system. By aligning the transducer on the sun in the early morning and setting both turntable and recorder going he could obtain complete records of the daily sunshine levels (including cloud shadowing effects).

Shortly before the eclipse was due he started making daily recordings to get some idea of how much I was varying day by day due to the change in the sun's declination. This variation day by day was found to be very small. That is, well below the random scatter of the points on the graph for any one day. On the day of the eclipse luck was with him and the sky was cloudless so that he obtained the recording shown in Table 4.18(c). By superimposing this graph of I against time obtained on the day of the eclipse onto that already obtained a few days previously he was able to make a moderately accurate estimate of the duration and nature of the eclipse.

Follow his procedure by superimposing the eclipse results for I against time onto your previous graph. Use the combined graph to calculate:

(8) The duration of the eclipse.

(9) The maximum percentage of the sun's disc covered by the moon.

(10) The Campbell–Stokes recorder is a glass sphere of diameter 4 inches and focal length 3 inches. The sensitive card is mounted outside it on its focal surface (the card is curved and is concentric with the sphere). Using this information sketch the layout of the recorder. Do you think that a design such as the student's recorder could replace the Campbell–Stokes type at seaside resorts? If not, why not?

Test Nineteen

The action of a sonic boom on a glass window

The recent supersonic flight trials by Concorde over the west coast of Great Britain have provided opportunities to study the environmental effects of sonic bangs generated by a supersonic transport aircraft. These flights have created some anxiety about the possible damage to old and historical buildings exposed to repeated sonic bangs.

As part of a general study of the effects of sonic bangs on building structures, the effects of bangs on leaded and stained glass windows is of particular interest because many of the windows have great artistic and historical value.

A sonic boom is a pressure pulse rather than a continuous sound wave and tends to excite the fundamental mode of a window rather than the higher frequency modes which do occur but with much lower amplitudes and energies. Because of the heavy damping involved the oscillations set up by the sonic boom die away quite rapidly, but the amplitudes produced may be sufficient to shatter the window. Considerable theoretical and experimental work has been carried out concerning the natural frequencies of glass windows and this test will deal with the early experiments on ordinary glass windows.

It has been shown by Warburton that the expression for the natural frequency f of a glass plate which is simply supported on all four edges is given by,

$$f = \frac{h\pi}{4\sqrt{3}} \left[\left(\frac{M}{a}\right)^2 + \left(\frac{N}{b}\right)^2 \right] \left[\frac{Eg}{\rho(1-\nu^2)} \right]^{\frac{1}{2}}$$

where E = Young's Modulus for the glass

ν = Poisson's ratio for the glass

ρ = density of the glass

h = thickness of the glass plate

g = acceleration due to gravity

a, b = horizontal and vertical lengths of the sides of the glass plate respectively

and M, N = number of half wave-lengths in the horizontal and vertical directions respectively

In the case of the fundamental frequency $M = N = 1$ and the equation becomes:

$$f = \frac{h\pi}{4\sqrt{3}} \left[\frac{1}{a^2} + \frac{1}{b^2} \right] \left[\frac{Eg}{\rho(1-\nu^2)} \right]^{\frac{1}{2}}$$

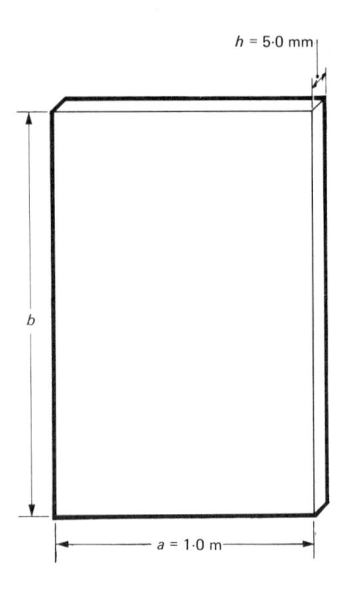

Fig. 4.19 The window.

$\nu = 0.22$
$\rho = 2.58 \times 10^3$ kg m^{-3}
$g = 9.81$ m s^{-2}

Fundamental frequency f, (Hz)	Vertical length b, (m)
191.4	0.50
106.4	0.75
76.6	1.00
62.8	1.25
55.1	1.50
50.9	1.75
47.9	2.00

Table 4.19.

An experiment was carried out in which a window was supported in a frame in accordance with the standard building practice in a wall of a building. The window was set vibrating over a range of frequencies using a variable frequency electrodynamic exciter, and from the response of the window its fundamental frequency was obtained. During the experiment a was kept constant at 1·0 m and the value of b was varied. The thickness h of the plates used was 5·0 mm. (See Fig. 4.19). The results of the experiment are given in Table 4.19 together with the values of the required constants.

Plot a graph of the fundamental frequency f as ordinate against $1/b^2$ as abscissa. From the slope of your graph obtain a value for the Young's Modulus E of the glass. Answer the following questions:

(1) Obtain the formula for the fundamental frequency of a glass window when b is very much greater than the fixed value of $a = 1.0$ m and indicate on your graph where this equation is applicable. Using this formula calculate the fundamental frequency of such a window whose width $a = 0.1$ m with all the other dimensions being as previously given and using the value of E just obtained.

(2) How does the fundamental frequency f change as b tends to zero? Does the trend of the graph confirm this?

(3) Use Warburton's equation to calculate the fundamental frequency for a glass window of dimensions $a = 0.5$ m and $b = 4.0$ m with all the other dimensions being as previously given. Would you expect to obtain the same frequency for a church window, of the same overall dimensions, comprising a large number of small panes joined together with lead strips? If not, would the frequency be higher or lower than that for the single glass pane? Give reasons for your answer.

(4) Sketch the nodal lines on a window of dimensions $a = 1.0$ m and $b = 2.0$ m for the following cases:

(a) $M = 1 \quad N = 1$

(b) $M = 2 \quad N = 1$

(c) $M = 1 \quad N = 3$

(d) $M = 2 \quad N = 2$

(5) St. David's Cathedral has a roof made of lead and heavy timbers and Truro Cathedral has a roof of tiles and lighter timbers, both roofs having approximately the same main frequency. If both cathedrals are subjected to identical sonic bangs which roof do you think would experience the greater vibration and why?

(6) Concorde produces a single heavy sonic boom whereas military supersonic aircraft generally produce a double boom. Why is this and how would you expect the intensities from the two types of aircraft to compare?

Test Twenty

A cylindrical rocking chair

An engineer in the course of his work was dealing with a problem involving the oscillation of a weighted cylinder on a horizontal plane. This set him thinking about the mechanics of the conventional rocking chair, in particular its stability and period of oscillation. He came to the conclusion that these chairs generally have a natural frequency of around one second unloaded and that when the sitter rocks the chair he does so at a frequency below the resonant value. That is, at somewhere between one half and one third of an oscillation per second (period of two to three seconds). This made him wonder whether a totally new form of chair could be made based on the cylindrical shape which would have a period in the range of two to four seconds so that the sitter would rock it at its resonant frequency and little effort would be required to maintain the oscillation.

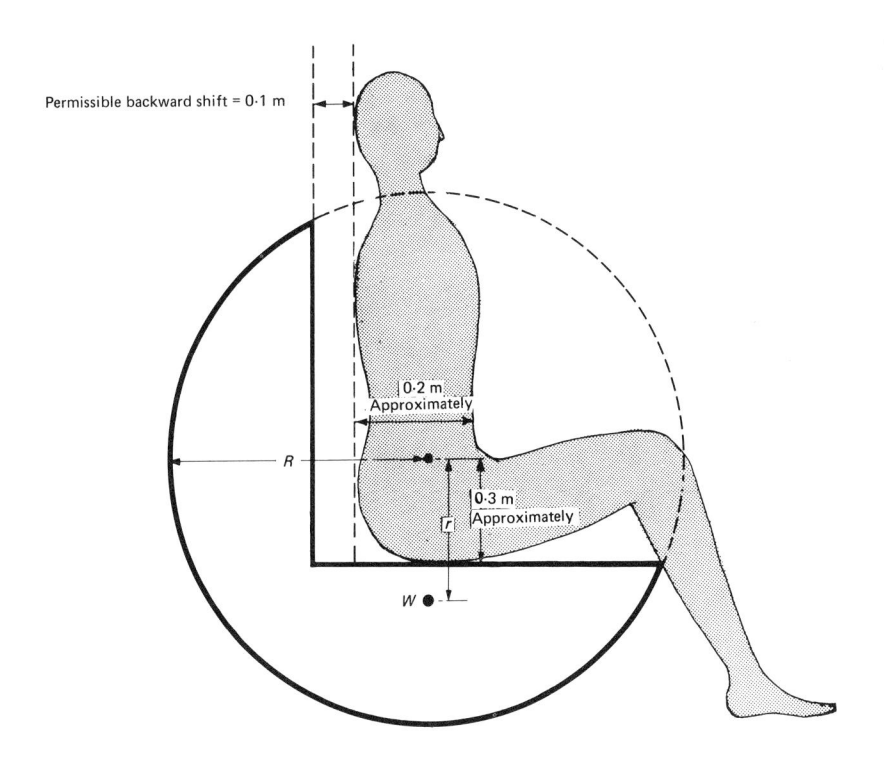

Fig. 4.20(a) Cylindrical rocking chair.

After some thought he settled on the shape shown in Fig. 4.20(a) where the seat height is chosen to get the sitter's centre of mass approximately on the cylinder axis. This simplifies the mathematics of the problem. Other assumptions he made were:

(a) the chair itself is very light (perhaps made of fibre glass) so that its moment of inertia during the oscillation may be ignored

(b) it is stabilised by a heavy bar beneath the seat and the whole mass of the system can be considered to be that of the bar w plus that of the sitter M

(c) in calculating the period of oscillation the sitter is treated as a cylinder of height 0·75 m and diameter 0·3 m. This gives him a moment of inertia about the axis of the chair of $Mk^2 = 0·2 M$ (his radius of gyration $k = 0·4$ m).

With these assumptions the engineer produced the following formula for the period of oscillation T:

$$T = 2\pi \sqrt{\frac{MR^2 + M \times 0·2 + w(R-r)^2}{wgr}}$$

or

$$T^2 = \frac{4\pi^2}{g}\left[\frac{M}{wr}(R^2+0·2)+\frac{R^2}{r}-2R+r\right]$$

where R is the radius of the cylindrical shape, r the distance of the heavy bar from the sitter's centre of mass and g is the acceleration due to gravity.

He saw from this formula that there were really three variables to consider, R, r and w (M cannot be considered as a variable here since he would have to consider the heaviest person likely to use the chair and put $M = 100$ kg).

He next considered if the chair would be stable. Using Fig. 4.20(b) he decided that if the sitter slid back from the central position by a maximum of 0·1 m the tilt produced should not exceed 20° for comfort. Applying the principle of moments to this diagram gives,

$$Mgy \cos\theta = wgr \sin\theta \text{ at balance.}$$

Therefore
$$y = \frac{w}{M} r \tan\theta$$

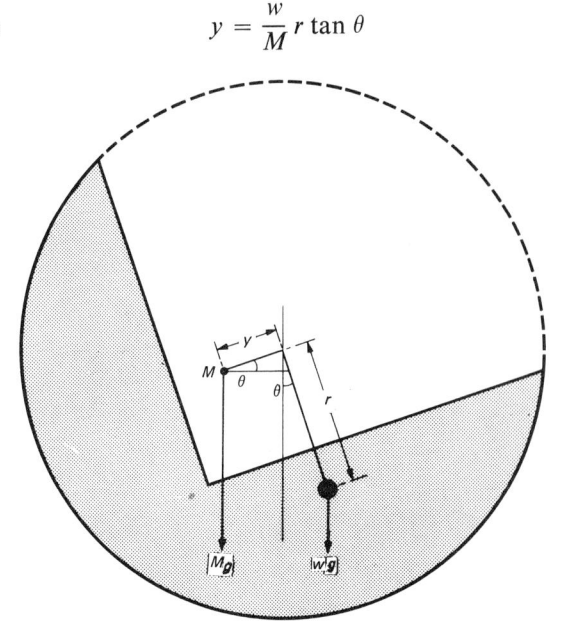

Fig. 4.20(b) Stability diagram.

	$T = 1.0$ s	$T = 2.0$ s	$T = 3.0$ s	$T = 4.0$ s	$T = 5.0$ s	Single root value of R
$r = 0.1$ m	R is Imaginary	$R = +0.197$ m -0.052 m	$R = +0.405$ -0.258	$R = +0.559$ -0.413	$R = +0.708$ -0.561	$R = 0.073$ m at $T = 1.740$ s
$r = 0.2$ m	Imaginary	$+0.263$ -0.029	$+0.510$ -0.277	$+0.725$ -0.491	$+0.910$ -0.678	$R = 0.116$ m at $T = 1.800$ s
$r = 0.3$ m	Imaginary	$+0.283$ $+0.015$	$+0.580$ -0.293	$+0.810$ -0.523	$+1.020$ -0.734	$R = 0.144$ m at $T = 1.895$ s
$r = 0.4$ m	Imaginary	$+0.274$ $+0.052$	$+0.620$ -0.293	$+0.868$ -0.541	$+1.090$ -0.765	$R = 0.163$ m at $T = 1.965$ s
$r = 0.5$ m	Imaginary	Imaginary	$+0.638$ -0.283	$+0.900$ -0.546	$+1.140$ -0.784	$R = 0.177$ m at $T = 2.060$ s

Table 4.20.

If $y = 0.1$ m and $\theta = 20°$ (tan $20° = 0.364$) this gives,

$$\frac{M}{w} = 3.64\,r$$

This result made him dubious about the design since it implies that w is going to be rather large, but he continued the analysis by putting

$$\frac{M}{w} = 3.64\,r$$

in to the formula for the period. This becomes,

$$T^2 = \frac{4\pi^2}{g}\left(3.64\,R^2 + 0.728 + \frac{R^2}{r} - 2R + r\right)$$

He then decided to find what chair radius R would be required to give various known values of T if the weight bar were placed at various positions. That is, he solved the quadratic equation for R inserting various values of T and r. The results are shown in Table 4.20.

He plotted a graph of R against T for each value of r using only the positive values and the single root value of R. He used this graph to come to some conclusions about the size, weight and practicability of the chair.

Plot this graph of R against T as described above and use it to answer questions 1 and 2.

(1) Write down the possible radii of the chair to give a period of 3·5 s for the permissible range of weight bar positions (values of r).
(2) There are two reasons why the engineer did not find the values of R for T greater than 5·0 s. The trend of the graph shows the physical reason. Explain this. The other reason is psychological. Comment on it.
(3) In considering the stability the engineer did not take into account any forward tilt produced by forward motion of the sitter. Would such forward motion obey the same equation as backward motion?
(4) Would a backward tilt of 20° be comfortable? Would a forward tilt of 20° be comfortable? If not what simple device could be fitted to the chair to restrict the angle of tilt?

(5) Using the permissible range of r calculate the values of w (mass of weight bar). Which of the radii in the answer to Question 1 corresponds to the lowest of these values for w?

(6) At first sight it appears that the maximum value of R is limited by the length of the back of the sitter's leg (0·6 m for most adults). What slight modification to the front of the chair would permit values of R greater than 0·6 m?

(7) What do you consider to be the most practical set of values for R, r and w, given that $T = 3\cdot5$ s?

(8) We have seen that the formula for T^2 can be written,

$$T^2 = \frac{4\pi^2}{g}\left(\frac{M}{wr}(R^2+0\cdot2)+\frac{(R-r)^2}{r}\right)$$

What form would this take on the assumption that $R = r$ and using

$$\frac{M}{w} = 3\cdot64\ r?$$

What period does the formula now predict for $R = 0$? Does this make physical sense? If not, try to show how the formula has broken down.

(9) It could be said that although this chair is an engineer's dream it could be a housewife's nightmare. Why do you think this is so?

Appendix

Answers, Comments and Graphs

Test one

(1) The student plotted the incorrect graph to verify the equation $h = \frac{1}{2}gt^2$. He should have plotted h against t^2 to give a straight line graph of slope $g/2$. Plotting h against t gives a parabola from which no useful information can be easily obtained

(2) (a) 0·1 s on the t axis is represented by $26\frac{2}{3}$ divisions making accurate plotting of points very difficult. A better choice would have been 0·1 s represented by 20 divisions

   (b) The scale along the h axis could easily be doubled

   (c) Units of h and t are not given

   (d) The points are dotted and not ringed or crossed for clarity

   (e) The graph has no title

Fig. A.1 Graph showing distance against (time)^2.

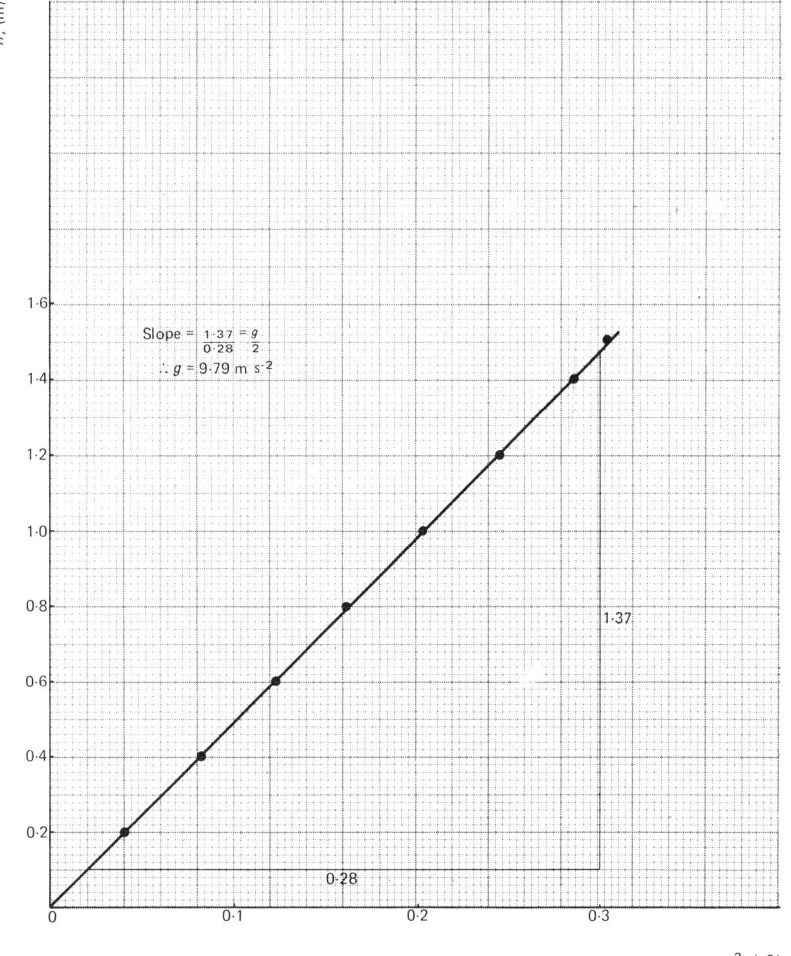

Distance h, (m)	(Time)^2 t^2, (s^2)
0·20	0·040
0·40	0·081
0·60	0·123
0·80	0·160
1·00	0·203
1·20	0·245
1·40	0·286
1·50	0·303

Table A.1.

(3) Table A.1 shows the values of h and t^2 which you should have plotted to give the graph in Fig. A.1. The measured value of g is 9·79 ms^{-2}

(4) If you measure the slope at $t = 0.5$ s on the student's graph you should find it to be approximately 4·9. The slope represents the velocity of the ball bearing at $t = 0.5$ s

Test two

The equation

$$T = 2\pi \sqrt{\frac{H-h}{g}}$$

has to be arranged in the form $y = mx + c$. This is done by squaring both sides and rearranging the equation,

$$T^2 = 4\pi^2 \frac{(H-h)}{g}$$

$$T^2 = -\frac{4\pi^2}{g} h + \frac{4\pi^2 H}{g}$$

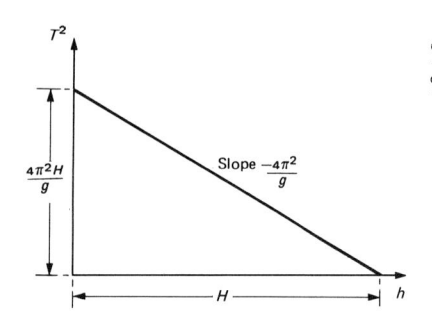

Fig. A.2(a) T^2 plotted against h.

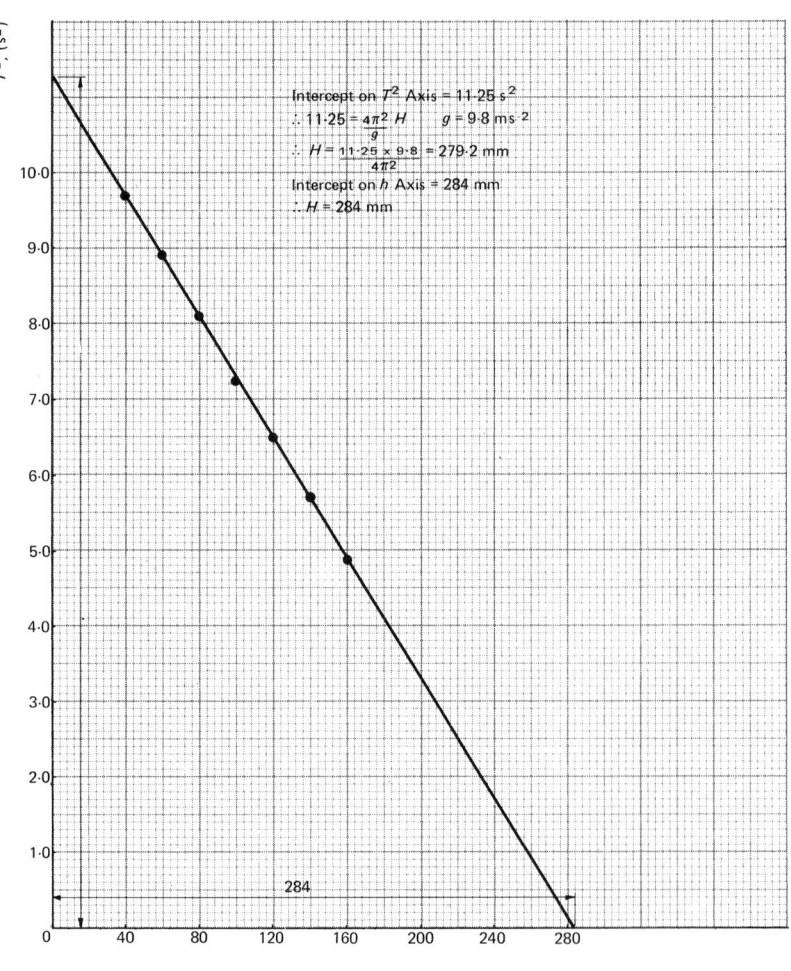

Fig. A.2(b) Graph of T^2 against h.

Intercept on T^2 Axis = 11·25 s^2
∴ 11·25 = $\frac{4\pi^2 H}{g}$ $g = 9.8$ ms^{-2}
∴ $H = \frac{11.25 \times 9.8}{4\pi^2} = 279.2$ mm
Intercept on h Axis = 284 mm
∴ $H = 284$ mm

(period)² (s²)	h (m)
9.65	0.40
8.86	0.60
8.09	0.80
7.18	1.00
6.49	1.20
5.68	1.40
4.88	1.60

Table A.2.

If T^2 is plotted as ordinate y and h as abscissa x we obtain a straight line graph of slope $-4\pi^2/g$. The intercept on the T^2 axis is obtained by putting $h = 0$ giving $4\pi^2 H/g$. The intercept on the h axis is obtained by putting $T^2 = 0$ giving H (see Fig. A.2(a)).

Table A.2 gives the values of T^2 and h and Fig. A.2(b) shows the graph you should have obtained. The value of H from the intercept on the T^2 axis is 279.2 mm and from the intercept on the h axis is. 284 mm.

(1) The intercept on the h axis gives the least accurate value for H because a large extrapolation has been used. A few larger values of h would help here

(2) In the derivation of the equation

$$T = 2\pi \sqrt{\frac{l}{g}}$$

the approximation $\sin \theta = \theta$ is made. This is only valid for angles less than about 10°

(3) The theory assumes that the bob is a point mass. Since in practice it is not, all distances must be measured to the centre of mass

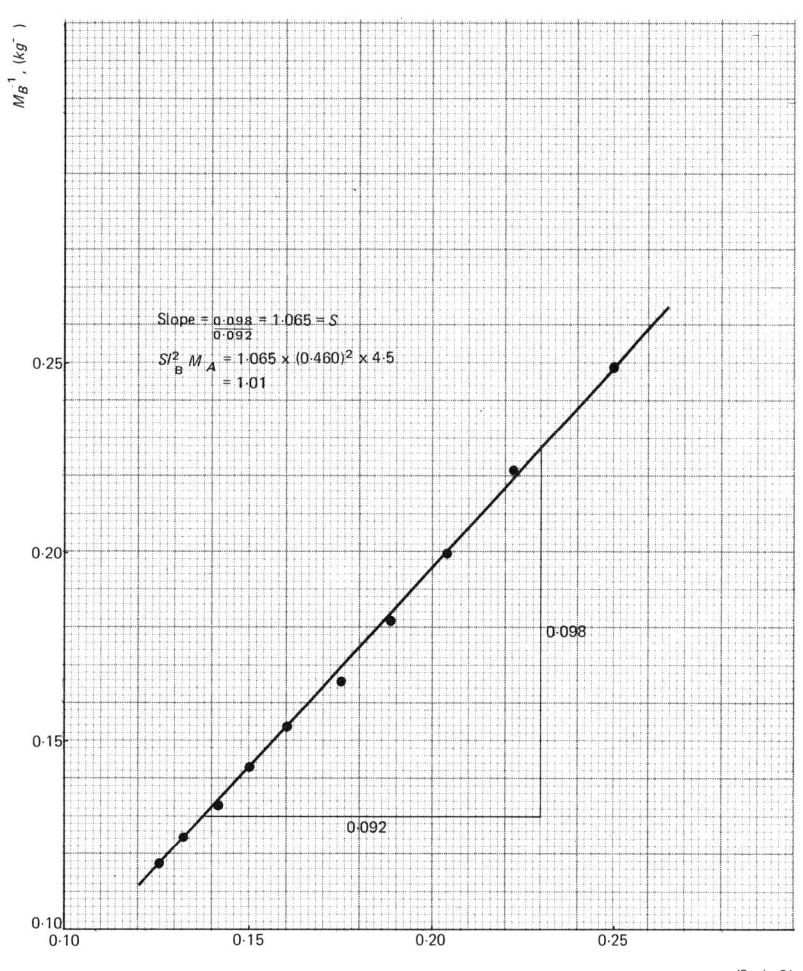

Fig. A.3 Graph of M_B^{-1} against l_A^2.

(4) By measuring 50 oscillations the fractional error in the period is greatly reduced

(5) The method has no practical application to the measurement of height. It is only intended to be an experimental exercise

Test three

The values of M_B^{-1} and l_A^2 are listed in Table A.3 and the graph of M_B^{-1} against l_A^2 is shown in Fig. A.3. The slope S of the graph is 1·065 and the value of $Sl_B^2 M_A$ is 1·01 which is very close to the theoretical value of unity.

(1) Using the equation

$$\frac{M_A}{l_A^2} = \frac{M_B}{l_B^2}$$

and putting $M_A = 4·5$ kg and $l_B = 0·46$ m we obtain,

$$\frac{4·5}{l_A^2} = \frac{M_B}{(0·46)^2}$$

Clearly M_B has its minimum value when l_A has its maximum value of 0·9 m. Therefore,

$$\frac{4·5}{(0·9)^2} = \frac{(M_B) \text{ min}}{(0·46)^2}$$

$$\therefore (M_B) \text{ min} = 1·18 \text{ kg}.$$

l_A takes its minimum value when M_B has its maximum value of 12·0 kg. Therefore,

$$\frac{4·5}{(l_A \text{ min})^2} = \frac{12·0}{(0·46)^2}$$

$$(l_A) \text{ min} = 0·282 \text{ m}.$$

M_B^{-1}, (kg^{-1})	l_A^2, (m²)
0·250	0·250
0·222	0·222
0·200	0·204
0·182	0·188
0·167	0·176
0·154	0·160
0·143	0·150
0·133	0·142
0·125	0·133
0·118	0·126

Table A.3.

Therefore the range of M_B is 1·2 kg to 12·0 kg and the corresponding range of l_A is 0·900 m to 0·282 m

(2) Results could have been taken for M_B in the range 8·5 kg to 12·0 kg corresponding to l_A of 0·355 m and 0·282 m, and in the range 1·2 kg to 4·0 kg for M_B and 0·900 m and 0·500 m for l_A. Therefore the parts of the graph where extra readings could have been taken are in the ranges,

(a) 0·118 kg^{-1} to 0·083 kg^{-1} for M_B^{-1}, corresponding to 0·126 m² to 0·079 m² for l_A^2

(b) 0·250 kg^{-1} to 0·833 kg^{-1} for M_B^{-1}, corresponding to 0·250 m² to 0·810 m² for l_A^2

(3) The fundamental frequency f_0 of a stretched wire is given by

$$f_0 = \frac{1}{2l}\sqrt{\frac{T}{m}}$$

$m = \pi r^2 \rho$ where r is the radius of the wire and ρ its density. Therefore,

$$f_0 = \frac{1}{2l}\sqrt{\frac{T}{\pi r^2 \rho}}$$

Therefore for the steel wire

$$(f_0)_s = \frac{1}{2l_s}\sqrt{\frac{T}{\pi r^2 \rho_s}}$$

and for the brass wire

$$(f_0)_b = \frac{1}{2l_b}\sqrt{\frac{T}{\pi r^2 \rho_b}}$$

Therefore $(f_0)_s/(f_0)_b = l_b\sqrt{\rho_b}/l_s\sqrt{\rho_s}$

But $(f_0)_s = (f_0)_b$ and $\rho_b = 1\cdot 1\,\rho_s$

Therefore $l_s = \sqrt{1\cdot 1}\,l_b$ and $l_s = 1\cdot 05\,l_b$

Therefore the lengths l_A are increased by the factor 1·05 if a brass wire is substituted for the steel wire. If the breaking stress for brass is half that of steel the maximum value for M_B is 6·0 kg. Therefore the possible range of values for l_A is from $0\cdot 420 \times 1\cdot 05 = 0\cdot 441$ m to 0·900 m

(4) When M_A is completely immersed in water the upthrust it experien-

$(u + v)$, (cm)	u, (cm)
100·0	11·0
64·2	12·0
53·7	13·0
48·0	14·0
44·0	15·0
42·8	16·0
41·7	17·0
41·0	18·0
40·6	19·0
40·6	20·0
40·6	21·0
41·2	22·0
42·4	25·0
43·3	27·0
45·7	30·0
49·6	35·0
54·0	40·0
58·8	45·0
63·4	50·0
68·2	55·0
72·8	60·0

Table A.4.

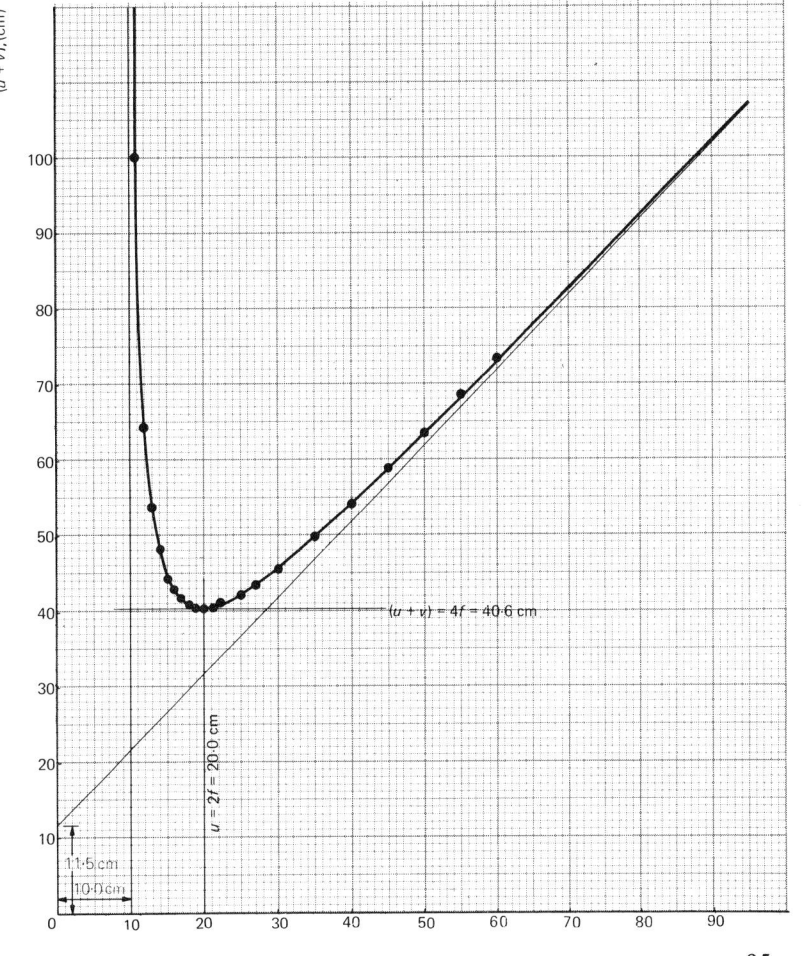

Fig. A.4 $(u + v)$ against u.

$\log_{10} D$	$\log_{10} L$
0·301	2·301
0·778	2·477
1·114	2·602
1·447	2·699
1·690	2·778
1·875	2·845
2·037	2·903

Table A.5.

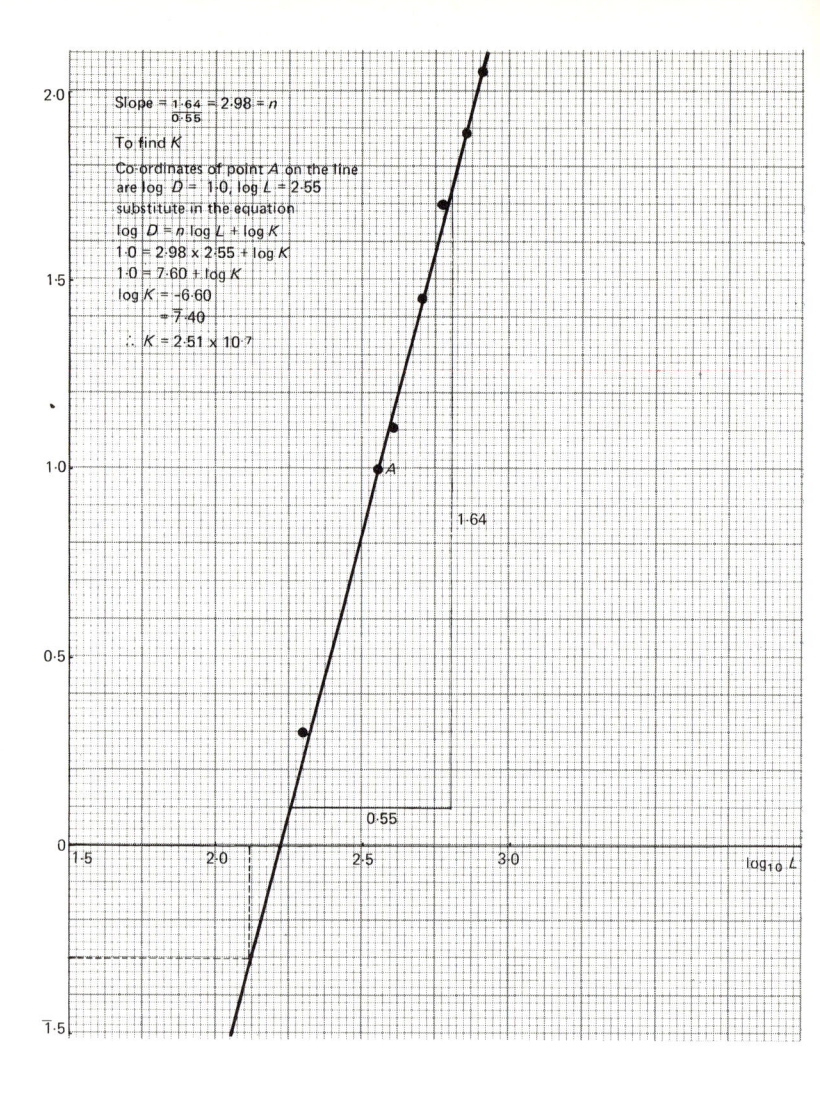

Slope $= \dfrac{1·64}{0·55} = 2·98 = n$

To find K

Co-ordinates of point A on the line are $\log D = 1·0$, $\log L = 2·55$ substitute in the equation
$\log D = n \log L + \log K$
$1·0 = 2·98 \times 2·55 + \log K$
$1·0 = 7·60 + \log K$
$\log K = -6·60$
$\quad = \bar{7}·40$
$\therefore K = 2·51 \times 10^{-7}$

Fig. A.5 Graph of $\log_{10} D$ against $\log_{10} L$.

ces will reduce the tension T in the wire, and hence the length l_A will have to be reduced to obtain unison again.

Test four

Table A.4 gives the results for $(u+v)$ and u and the graph is shown in Fig. A.4.

The minimum of the graph occurs at $(u+v) = 4f = 40·6$ cm giving $f = 10·2$ cm and at $u = 2f = 20·0$ cm giving $f = 10·0$ cm. The vertical asymptote crosses the u axis at $u = f = 10·0$ cm. The other asymptote cuts the $(u+v)$ axis at $(u+v) = f = 11·5$ cm.

(1) The maximum value of $(u+v)$ used was 100·0 cm. The experimenter therefore only used two thirds of the available optical bench length. However the extra values obtained would be at large values of $(u+v)$. Those for which u is very small and v very large would be unreliable since with v large it is difficult to judge the focussed position of the image (the image has large depth of focus). The values for which u is large and v is small would give extra points at the right hand end of the curve which would be useful.

$\log_{10} T$	$\log_{10} L$
0·041	1·477
0·152	1·699
0·225	1·845
0·279	1·954
0·324	0·041
0·360	0·114
0·391	0·176
0·418	0·230

Table A.6.

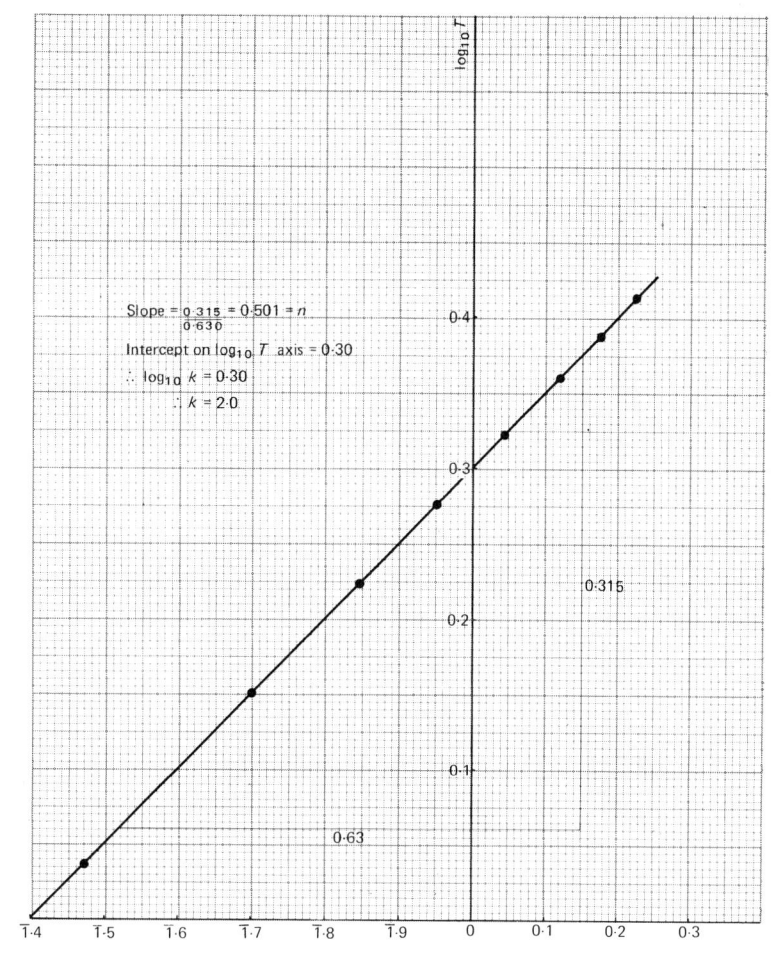

Fig. A.6 Graph of $\log_{10} T$ against $\log_{10} l$.

(2) It would have helped with the drawing of the asymptotes if more results had been taken for values of u in the regions 10·0 to 12·0 cm and 70·0 cm upwards. The point at $u = 22·0$ cm is off the drawn curve so that values of $(u+v)$ for $u = 23·0$ and 24·0 cm would have enabled the curve to be drawn with more certainty in this region.

(3) The minimum of the curve is fairly flat, therefore $(u+v) = 4f$ can be judged accurately, whereas $u = 2f$ is more difficult to judge. Although the asymptotes are tangents to the curve at infinity they are not difficult to draw accurately but the right hand one involves a very large extrapolation.

(4) If the object to screen distance is less than $4f$ no focussed real image can be formed on the screen (this is a basic property of a convex lens). If the distance is just less than $4f$ we would observe a slightly out of focus image.

Note

The validity of the experimental points can be checked when you remember that the object and the image positions are conjugate points for the lens. That is, numerical values of u and v are interchangeable. For example, at $u = 14.0$ cm, $v = 34.0$ cm we have $(u+v) = 48.0$ cm, then at $v = 14.0$ cm we ought to have $u = 34.0$ cm, but in fact the measured value is 40.0 cm. A number of pairs of results can be checked in this way, and an idea gained of their accuracies. We would expect to find that when v is large the accuracy is least for the reasons mentioned in the answer to Question 1.

Test five

Table A.5 gives the values for $\log_{10} D$ and $\log_{10} L$ and the graph is shown in Fig. A.5. The value of the slope n is 2·98 and $K = 2·51 \times 10^{-7}$. Since $\log_{10} D$ for $D = 0.5$ mm is $\bar{1}·6990$ the $\log_{10} D$ scale has been drawn to show bar numbers. The value of $\log_{10} L$ corresponding to $\log_{10} D = \bar{1}·699$ is 2·12. Hence $L = 131·8$ mm.

Test six

Table A.6 gives the values for $\log_{10} T$ and $\log_{10} l$ and Fig. A.6 shows the graph of $\log_{10} T$ against $\log_{10} l$. The value of the slope $n = 0·50$ and the intercept on the $\log_{10} T$ axis is $\log_{10} k = 0·30$. Therefore $k = 2·00$.

The formula $T = 2\pi\sqrt{l/g}$ can be written as $2\pi.l^{\frac{1}{2}}/\sqrt{g}$ where $k = 2\pi/\sqrt{g} = 2·01$ and $n = 0·5$.

Test seven

Table A.7 gives the values of IV and R and Fig. A.7 shows the graph of IV against R.

(1) We can express the total power EI as the sum of the external power I^2R and the internal power I^2r. That is, $EI = I^2R + I^2r$. If $R = 0$, $EI = I^2r$. That is, there is no external power developed. Even though I may be fairly large, V must be zero.

(2) Since the currents are quoted to $\pm 0·001$ A we may assume that the ammeter was calibrated to this accuracy. The range of the ammeter was probably 0 to 250 mA. Similarly the voltmeter readings are quoted to $\pm 0·01$ V and again we may assume that the voltmeter was calibrated to this accuracy. The range of the voltmeter was probably 0 to 1·5 V.

(3) The maximum power obtained is 0·113 W occurring at $R = 5·0\,\Omega$.

(4) Putting $R = r = 5\,\Omega$ we obtain

$$P = \frac{E^2 R}{4R^2} = \frac{E^2}{4R}$$

$$\therefore P = \frac{(1·5)^2}{20} = \frac{2·25}{20} = 0·1125 \text{ W}$$

The measured value is as near to this calculated value as the accuracy of the instruments allow.

(5) (a) When R is very large we can neglect r with respect to R so that

$$P = \frac{E^2 R}{R^2}$$

That is

$$P = \frac{E^2}{R}$$

Power IV, (W)	Resistance R, (Ω)
	0
0·063	1·0
0·094	2·0
0·104	3·0
0·108	4·0
0·113	5·0
0·111	6·0
0·109	7·0
0·107	8·0
0·103	9·0
0·100	10·0
0·095	12·0
0·084	15·0
0·072	20·0

Table A.7.

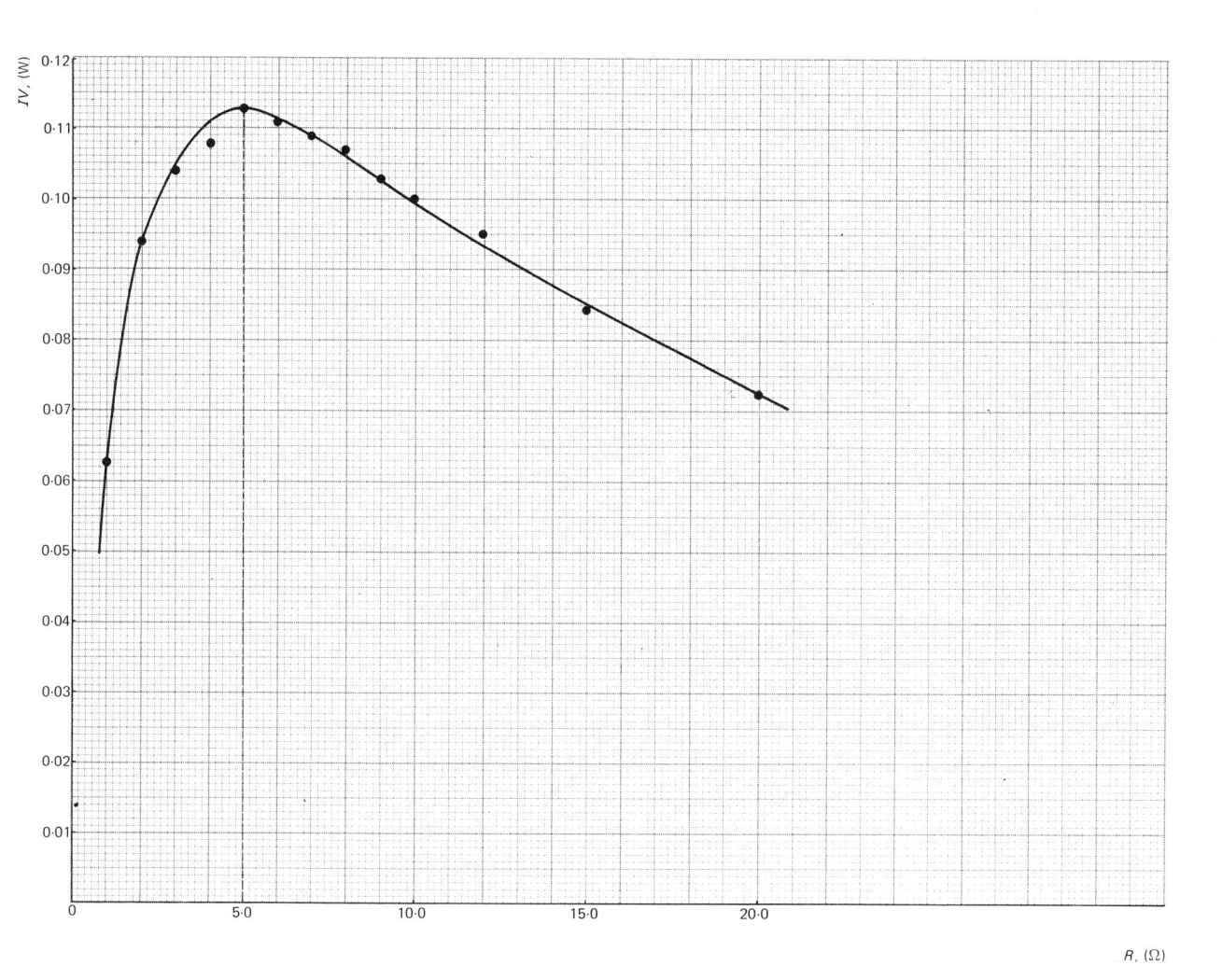

Fig. A.7 Power against resistance.

(b) When $R \to 0$ it can be neglected with respect to r. Therefore

$$P = \frac{E^2 R}{r^2}$$

so that $P \to 0$ as $R \to 0$. These results are confirmed by the trend of the graph.

(6) The general conclusion drawn from Question 4 is that maximum power is developed externally when the external load is equal to the internal resistance of the source. This idea is applicable to other forms of power supply. In fact it is one of the design problems in electronic circuits to match the impedance (a.c. resistance) of one stage of the circuit with that of the next to maximise the power transfer.

Test eight

The graphs of the resistance of the unknown component against temperature and the resistance of the copper coil against temperature are shown in Fig. A.8. They have been drawn on the same sheet to make the contrast between the two graphs more obvious.

(1) The student knew that a capacitor does not pass d.c. and therefore

Fig. A.8 Graphs of thermistor and copper coil resistances against temperature.

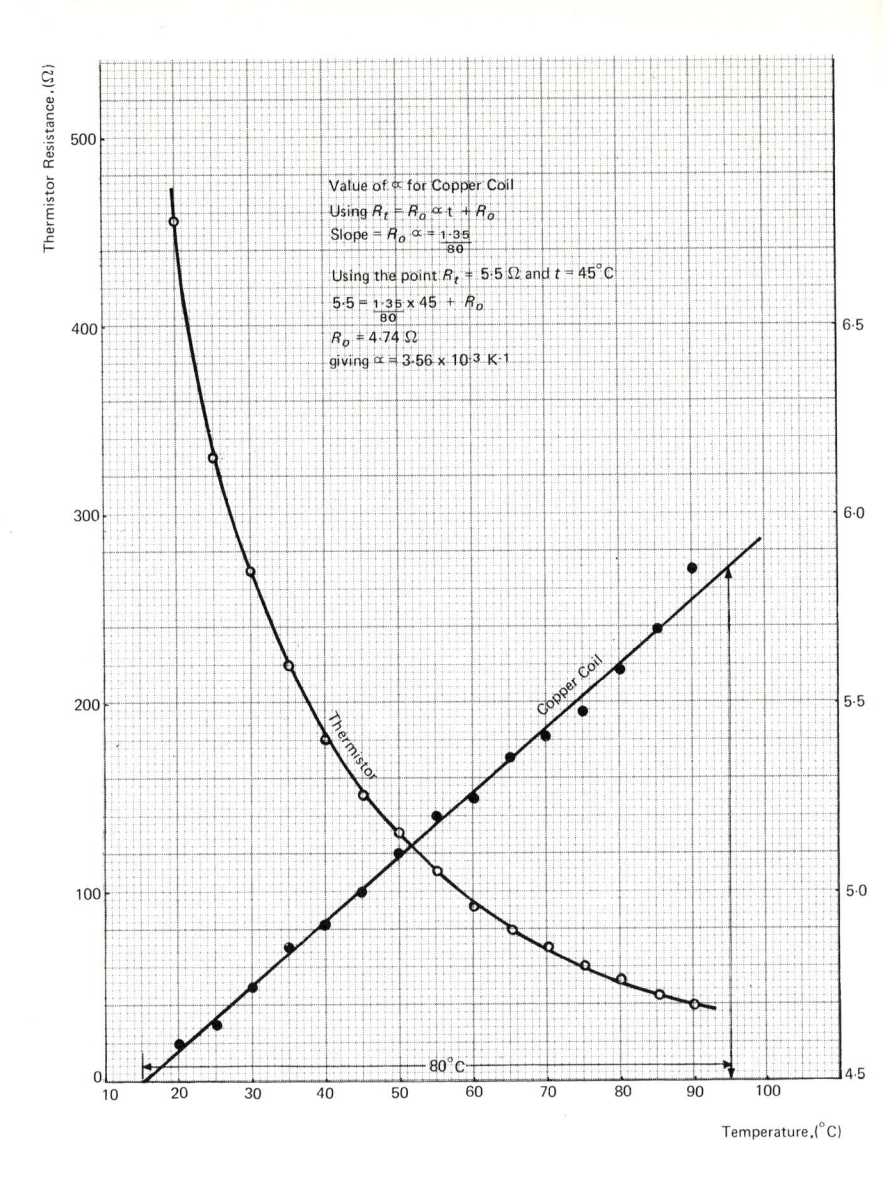

Value of α for Copper Coil
Using $R_t = R_o \alpha t + R_o$
Slope $= R_o \alpha = \frac{1 \cdot 35}{80}$
Using the point $R_t = 5 \cdot 5 \, \Omega$ and $t = 45°C$
$5 \cdot 5 = \frac{1 \cdot 35}{80} \times 45 + R_o$
$R_o = 4 \cdot 74 \, \Omega$
giving $\alpha = 3 \cdot 56 \times 10^{-3} \, K^{-1}$

has infinite d.c. resistance. The unknown components' d.c. resistance was measured to be 500 ohms and clearly is not a capacitor.

(2) The resistance temperature graph for copper is a straight line with a small positive slope which is typical of metals. The resistance temperature graph for the unknown component has a large negative variable slope.

(3) The temperature coefficient of resistance α has a value of

$$3 \cdot 56 \times 10^{-3} \, K^{-1}.$$

(4) R_0 is not measurable for the unknown component and the slope is not constant therefore such a definition cannot be used. A meaningful definition in this case would be,

$$\alpha = \frac{\text{slope (tangent to the curve)}}{\text{resistance at which slope is measured}}$$

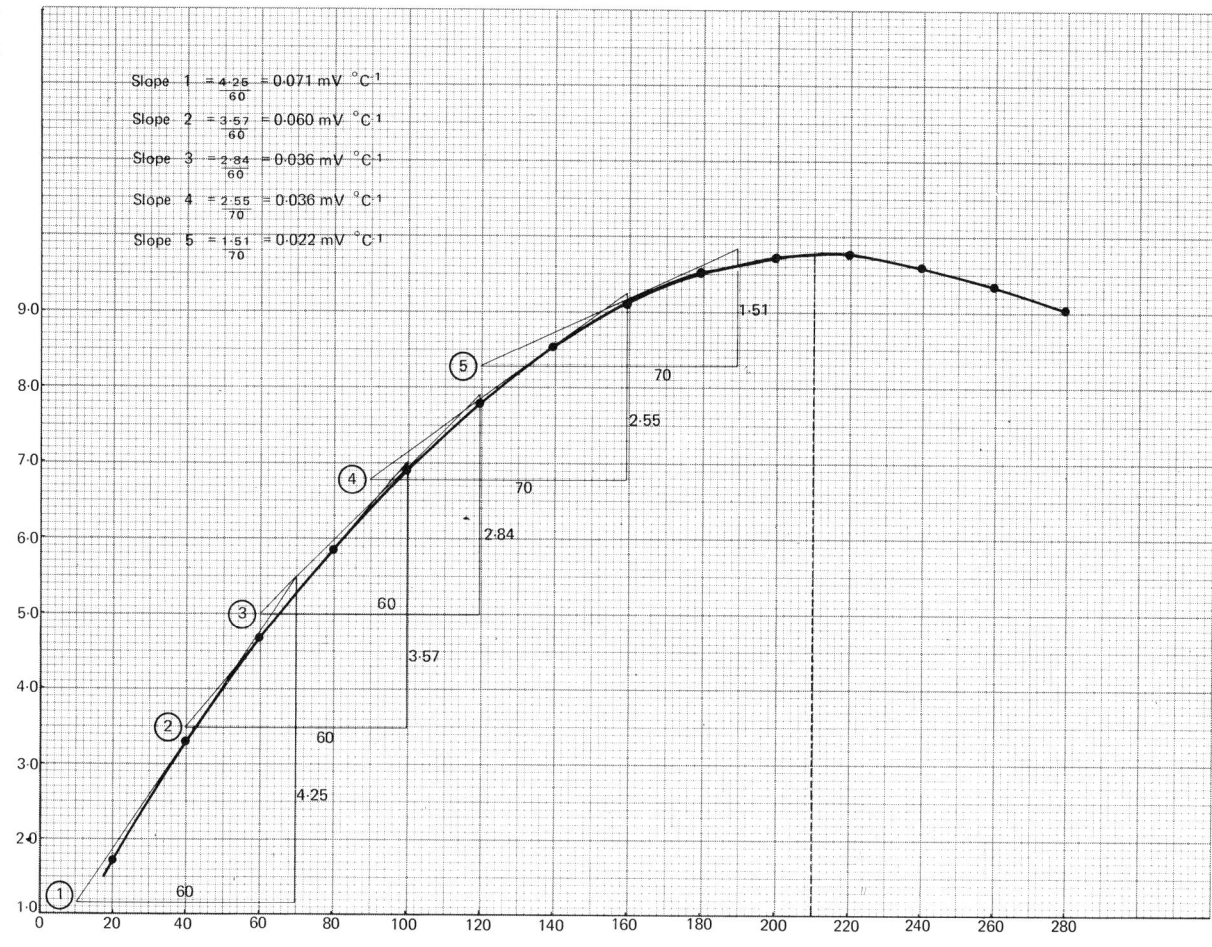

Slope 1 = 4·25/60 = 0·071 mV °C⁻¹
Slope 2 = 3·57/60 = 0·060 mV °C⁻¹
Slope 3 = 2·84/60 = 0·036 mV °C⁻¹
Slope 4 = 2·55/70 = 0·036 mV °C⁻¹
Slope 5 = 1·51/70 = 0·022 mV °C⁻¹

Fig. A.9(a) Graph of thermo-electric e.m.f. against temperature.

Test nine

(5) The student originally found the resistance of the unknown component to be 500 ohms at room temperature. If you extrapolate the graph for this component to above 500 ohms you should be able to read off from it a temperature of 19·5°C corresponding to this resistance. This is very approximate because it is very difficult to extrapolate a steep curve accurately.

(6) The ratio of the two resistance scales is 200:1 which accounts for the larger apparent scatter on the copper coil graph.

The graph of E against t is shown in Fig. A.9(a).

(1) From the graph the neutral temperature is about 210°C. However with such a flattened curve it is difficult to judge the maximum exactly and we would not claim a better accuracy than ± 5°C. Therefore the neutral temperature is 210 ± 5°C.

(2) In the equation $E = at + bt^2$, t is the temperature difference between the hot and the cold junctions. If the cold junction had been maintained at 50°C then the e.m.f. E produced when the hot junction is at 90°C is equal to the value of the e.m.f. at 90°C (E_{90}) minus the

101

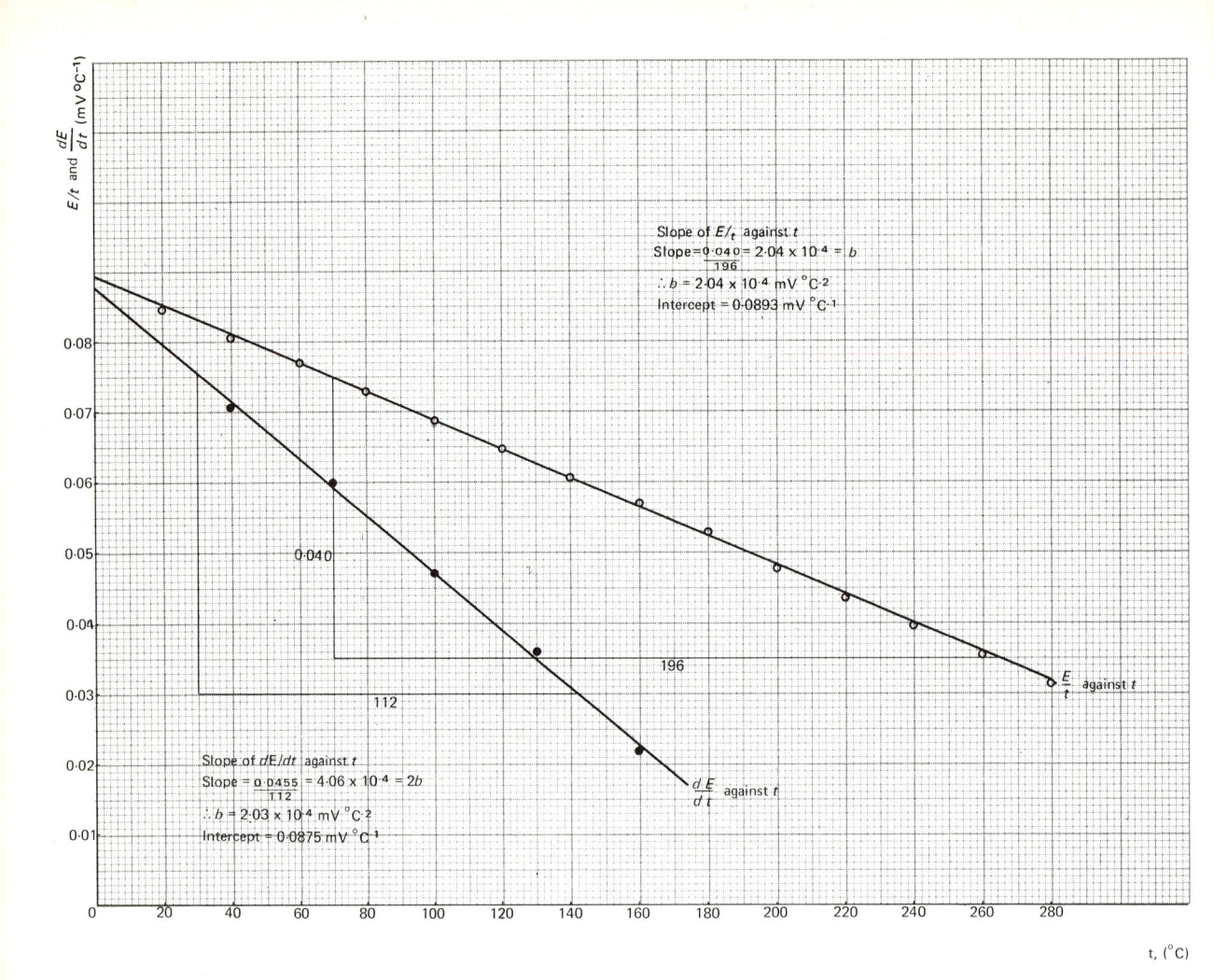

Fig. A.9(b) Graphs of dE/dt against t and E/t against t.

value of the e.m.f. at 50°C (E_{50}) taken from the graph in Fig. A.9(a) with the cold junction at 0°C

$$E_{90} = 6\cdot 38 \text{ mV}, \quad E_{50} = 3\cdot 95 \text{ mV}$$

$$E = E_{90} - E_{50} = 2\cdot 43 \text{ mV}$$

(3) Table A.9(a) shows the values of dE/dt for various temperatures of the hot junction. The graph of dE/dt against t is shown in Fig. A.9(b). The graph has the form of $y = mx + c$ with slope equal to $2b$ and an intercept on the dE/dt axis equal to a. $b = 2\cdot 03 \times 10^{-4}$ mV °C^{-2} and $a = 0\cdot 088$ mV °C^{-1}. The scatter of your points is due partly to the difficulty in drawing the curve and partly to the problem of drawing tangents accurately.

(4) $$E = at + bt^2$$

Dividing both sides by t gives,

$$\frac{E}{t} = a + bt$$

dE/dt, (mV °C^{-1})	t, (°C)
0·071	40
0·060	70
0·047	100
0·036	130
0·022	160

Table A.9(a).

E/t, (mV °C^{-1})	t, (°C)
0·085	20
0·081	40
0·077	60
0·073	80
0·069	100
0·065	120
0·061	140
0·057	160
0·053	180
0·048	200
0·044	220
0·040	240
0·036	260
0·032	280

Table A.9(b).

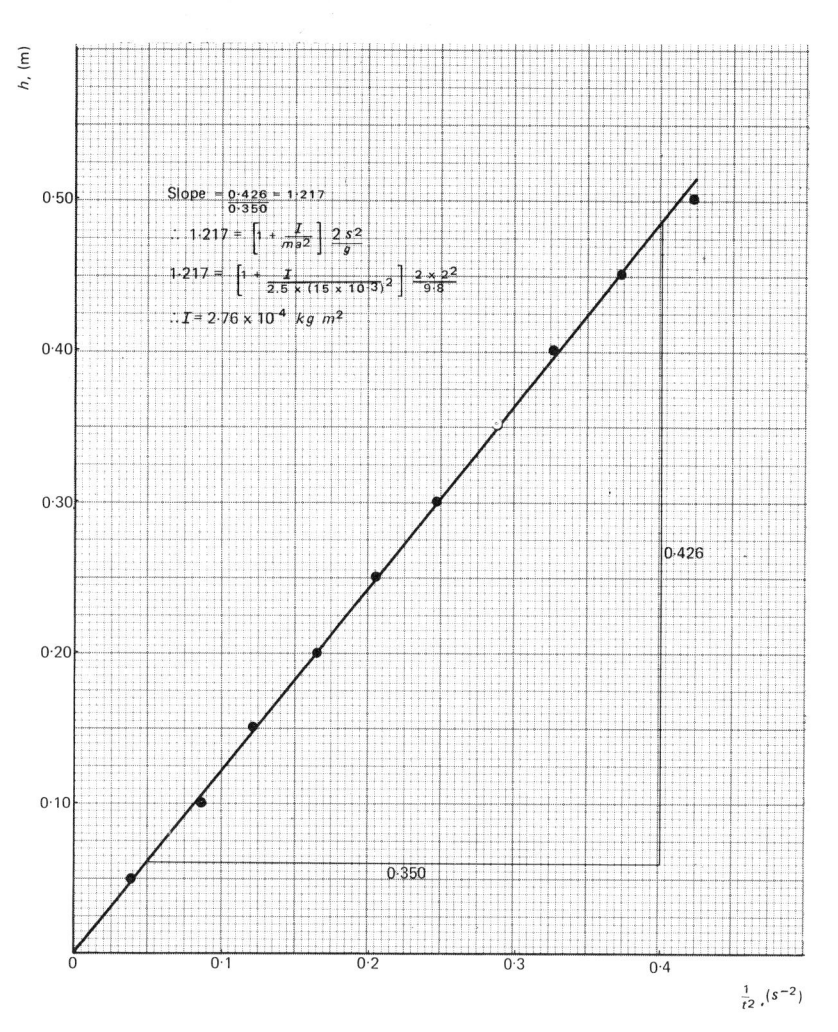

Fig. A.10 Graph of h against $1/t^2$.

h, (m)	$1/t^2$, (s^{-2})
0·05	0·040
0·10	0·085
0·15	0·120
0·20	0·166
0·25	0·205
0·30	0·245
0·35	0·286
0·40	0·326
0·45	0·372
0·50	0·421

Table A.10.

which is now in the form $y = mx + c$ where $y = E/t$ and $x = t$. The graph of E/t against t is shown in Fig. A.9(b) which has a slope $b = 2·04 \times 10^{-4}$ mV °C^{-2} and an intercept a on the E/t axis of $0·089$ mV °C^{-1}. The values obtained from this graph are probably more reliable since the drawing of the graph did not involve a curve with tangents to it. (Values of E/t and t are shown in Table A.9(b)).
(5) The neutral temperature is about 210°C. If the thermocouple was used above this temperature it would give ambiguous readings. For example an e.m.f. of 9·00 mV could correspond to a hot junction temperature of either 278°C or 156°C. To avoid such ambiguities a couple should not be used above its neutral temperature.

Test ten

The equation
$$2gh = \left(\frac{2s}{t}\right)^2 + \frac{I}{ma^2}\left(\frac{2s}{t}\right)^2$$

can be rearranged in the form,

$$h = \frac{1}{t^2}\left[1 + \frac{I}{ma^2}\right]\frac{2s^2}{g}$$

Slope $= \dfrac{0·426}{0·350} = 1·217$

$\therefore 1·217 = \left[1 + \dfrac{I}{ma^2}\right]\dfrac{2s^2}{g}$

$1·217 = \left[1 + \dfrac{I}{2·5 \times (15 \times 10^{-3})^2}\right]\dfrac{2 \times 2^2}{9·8}$

$\therefore I = 2·76 \times 10^{-4}$ kg m^2

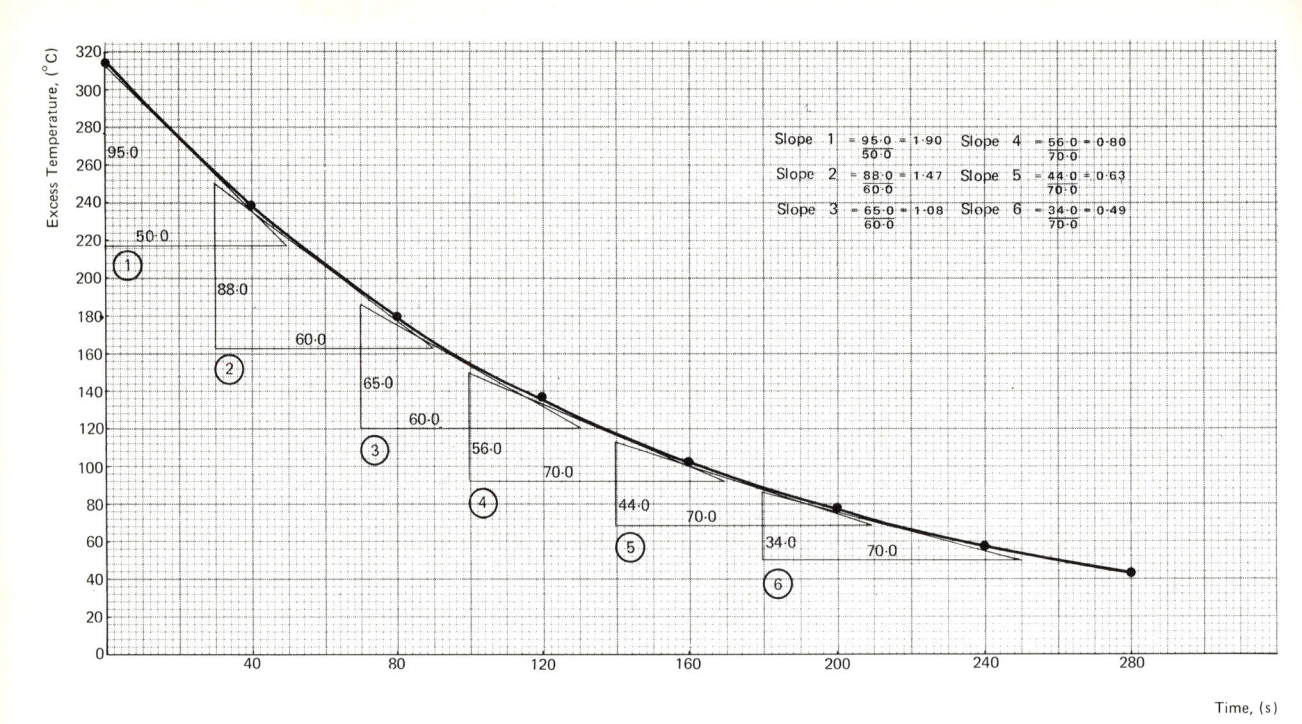

Fig. A.11 (a) Excess temperature against time.

Slope 1 = $\frac{95.0}{50.0}$ = 1.90   Slope 4 = $\frac{56.0}{70.0}$ = 0.80

Slope 2 = $\frac{88.0}{60.0}$ = 1.47   Slope 5 = $\frac{44.0}{70.0}$ = 0.63

Slope 3 = $\frac{65.0}{60.0}$ = 1.08   Slope 6 = $\frac{34.0}{70.0}$ = 0.49

Therefore if h is plotted against $1/t^2$ a straight line graph passing through the origin is obtained having a slope of

$$\left[1+\frac{I}{ma^2}\right]\frac{2s^2}{g}$$

The Table A.10 gives the values of h and $1/t^2$ and Fig. A.10 shows the corresponding graph.

(1) If there is no rotation the potential energy lost equals the kinetic energy of translation gained. That is,

$$mgh = \tfrac{1}{2}mv_s^2$$

where v_s is the sliding velocity after distance s. Clearly v_s is greater than v in the original equation for rolling motion and the time taken to cover a distance s is less.

(2) Frictional force between the body and the inclined plane. If this force is big enough to prevent relative motion between the surface of the body and the plane the body can only move down the plane by rolling.

(3) The lower half of the cylinder rotates in the opposite direction to the motion of the cylinder axis, whilst the upper half rotates in the same direction. Therefore the upper part moves appreciably while the exposure is being made whereas the lower part does not. In fact the part of the cylinder in contact with the plane is momentarily at rest.

Test eleven

The graph of excess temperature against time is shown in Fig. A.11(a).
(1) Tangents have been drawn to the cooling curve at difference excess temperatures as shown and their slopes $d\theta/dt$ have been measured. The values of $d\theta/dt$ and the corresponding excess temperatures are

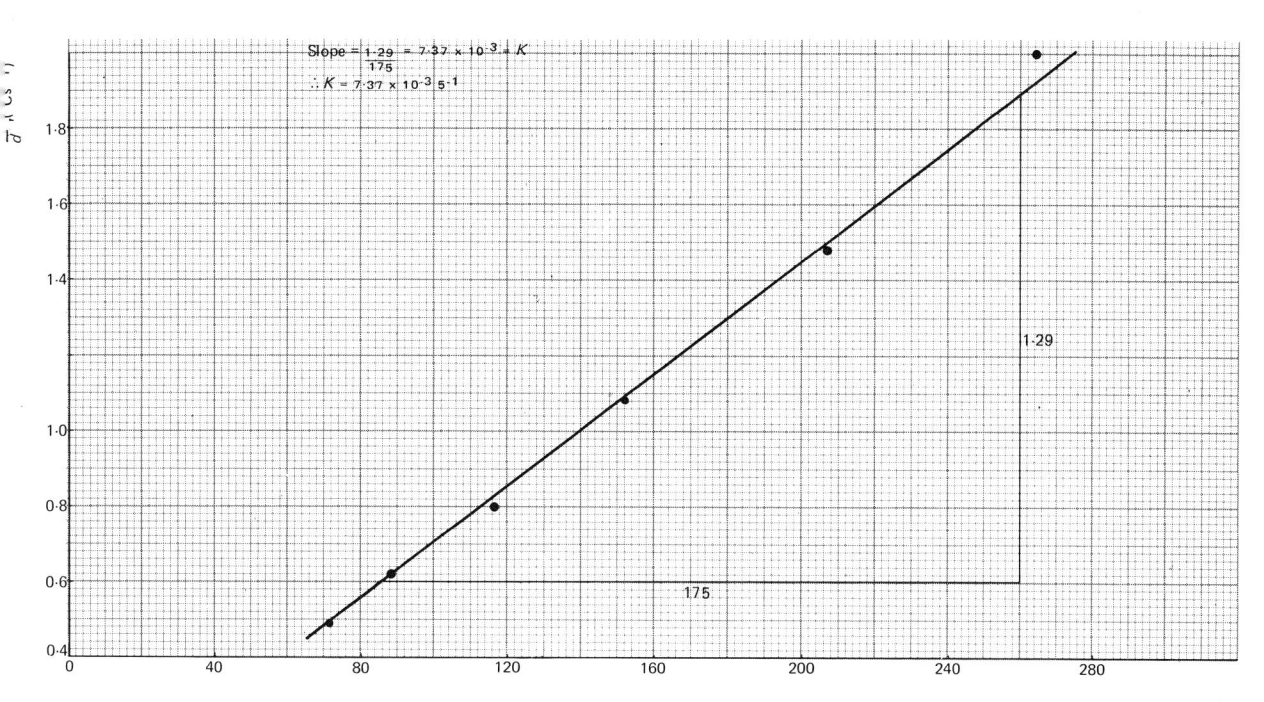

Fig. A.11(b) $d\theta/dt$ against excess temperature.

Excess Temperature, (°C)

Fig. A.11(c) Excess temperature against time for different draught speeds.

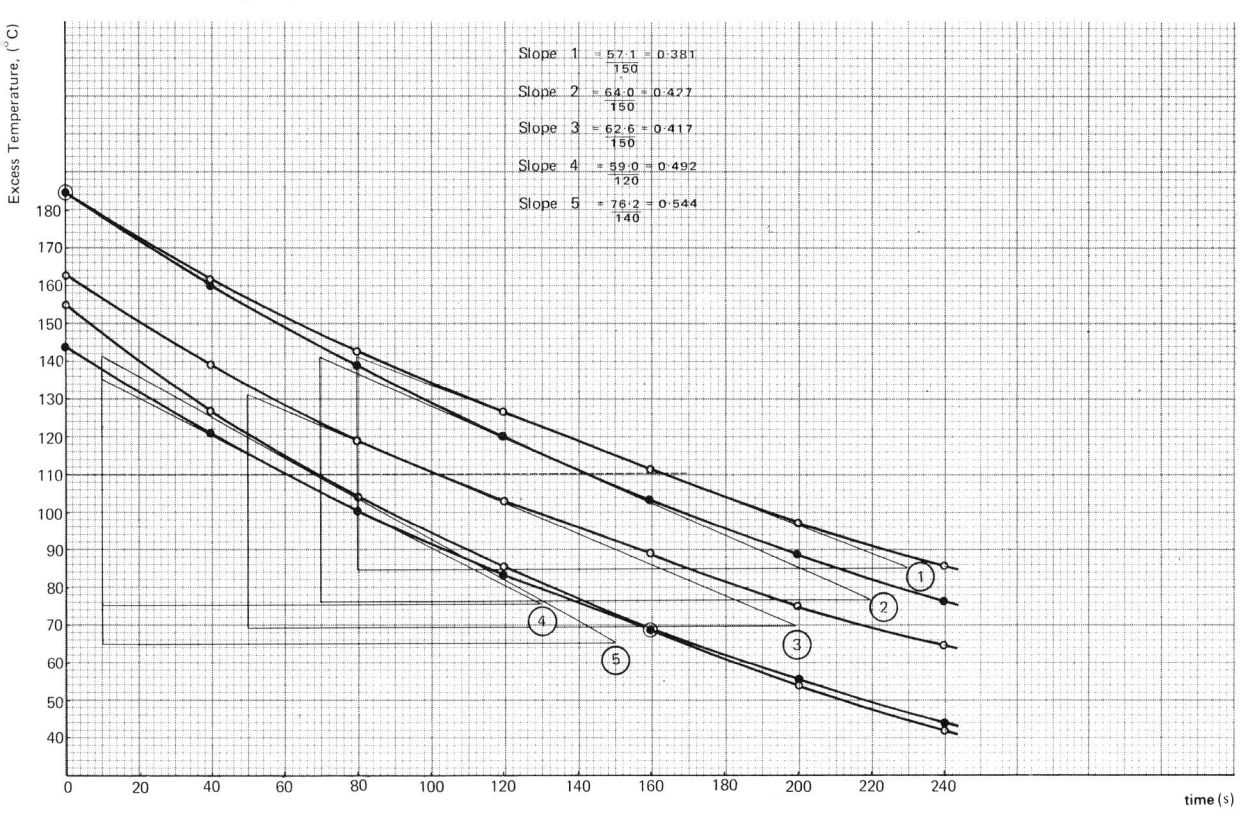

Slope 1 = $\frac{57.1}{150}$ = 0.381

Slope 2 = $\frac{64.0}{150}$ = 0.427

Slope 3 = $\frac{62.6}{150}$ = 0.417

Slope 4 = $\frac{59.0}{120}$ = 0.492

Slope 5 = $\frac{76.2}{140}$ = 0.544

time (s)

105

Fig. A.11(d) Draught speed against $d\theta/dt$.

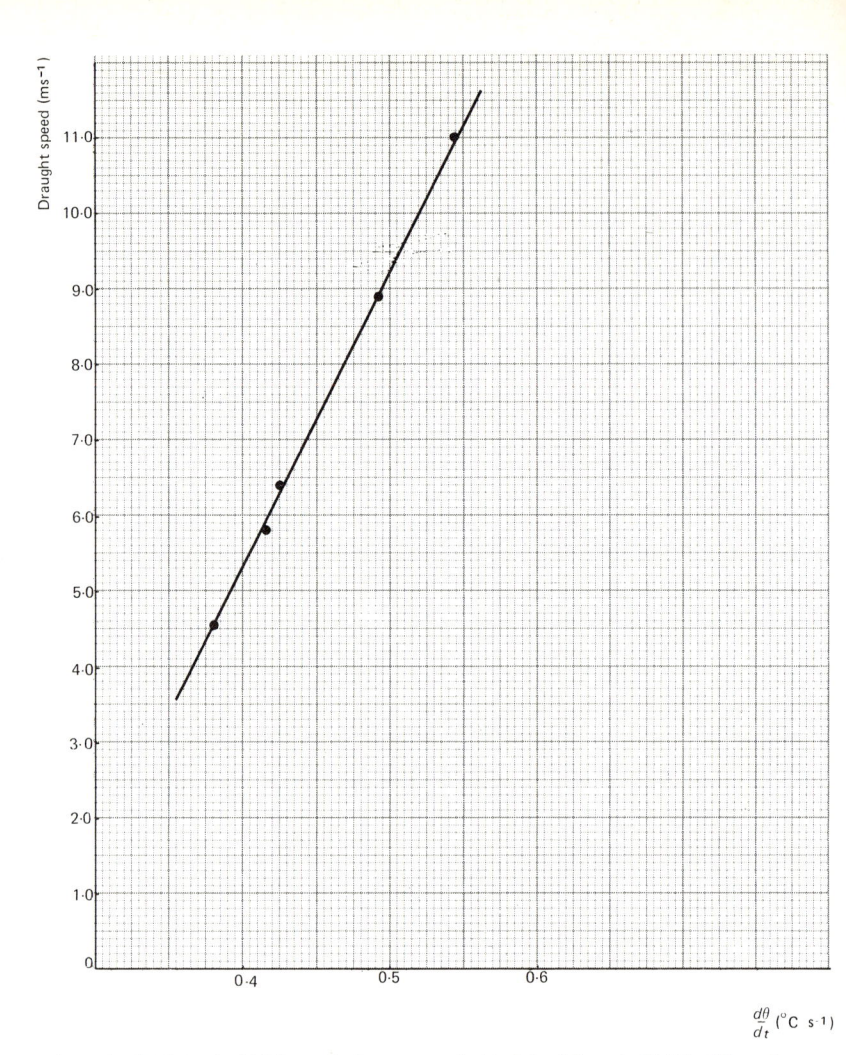

$d\theta/dt$, (°C s^{-1})	Excess temperature, (°C)
1·90	264
1·47	206
1·08	152
0·80	116
0·63	88
0·49	71

Table A.11(a).

Draught speed (ms^{-1})	$d\theta/dt$ at 110°C (°C s^{-1})
4·6	0·381
5·8	0·417
6·4	0·427
8·9	0·492
11·0	0·544

Table A.11(b).

given in Table A.11(a) and they are plotted in Fig. A.11(b). The slope K of this graph has the value of $7\cdot37 \times 10^{-3}$ s^{-1}. If Newton's law of cooling is obeyed the line must pass through the origin and have the equation,

$$\frac{d\theta}{dt} = 7\cdot37 \times 10^{-3}(\theta - \theta_0)$$

To check whether the line passes through the origin we choose any point on the line, for example (0·71, 100) and substitute its coordinates into the equation to give, $0\cdot71 = 7\cdot37 \times 10^{-3}\cdot(100)$ that is, $0\cdot71 = 0\cdot737$. There is sufficient agreement between these two values to conclude that the line almost passes through the origin and hence the graph shows that Newton's law of cooling is approximately obeyed.

(2) If the surface of the cylinder had been blackened we would expect the slope to be greater since a blackened surface is a more efficient radiator than a polished one at the same temperature and will therefore lose energy at a greater rate.

The cooling curves for the different draught speeds have been plotted in Fig. A.11(c). Tangents have been drawn to each of the

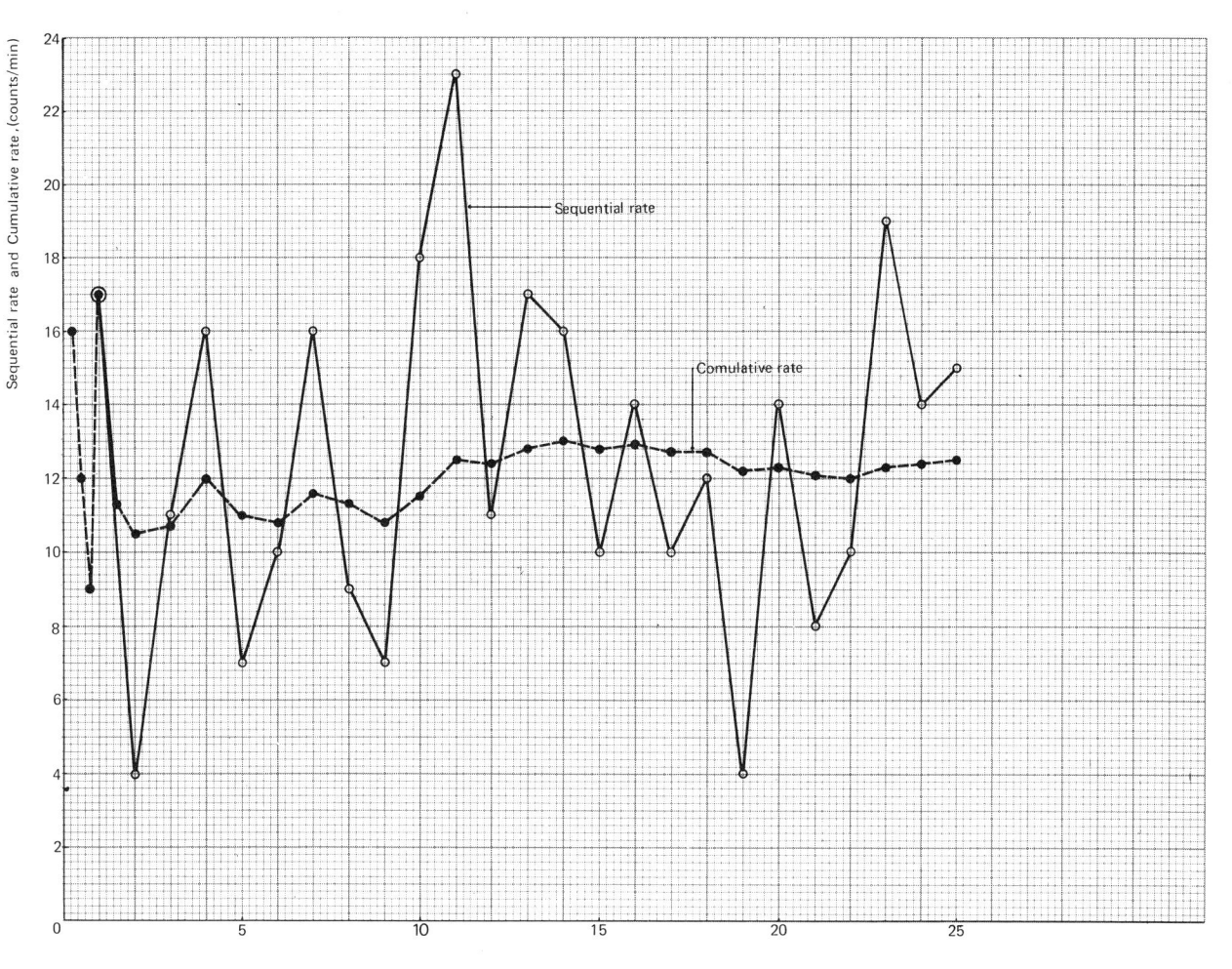

Fig. A.12 Sequential rate and cumulative rate against time.

curves at an excess temperature of 110°C and their slopes $d\theta/dt$ measured. (See Table A.11(b)). A plot of draught speed against $d\theta/dt$ is shown in Fig. A.11(d) and is a straight line. It is fairly obvious that this line does not pass through the origin and that it has an intercept on the $d\theta/dt$ axis for zero draught speed. Hence we can conclude that the rate of cooling is proportional to the draught speed plus a constant. This constant will be the rate of cooling which occurs at zero draught speed.

Test twelve

The completed count rate table is shown as Table A.12 and the graphs of these results are shown in Fig. A.12.

(1) As was explained to you in the introductory theory of the problem, radioactive decay is a random process and there is a wide variation in sequential one minute counts. The graph shows this effect quite strikingly, the maximum and minimum count rates being 23 per minute and 4 per minute. Using these values we obtain percentage accuracies of

$$\frac{100}{\sqrt{23}} = 21\% \quad \text{and} \quad \frac{100}{\sqrt{4}} = 50\%$$

Elapsed time (minutes)	Total counts	Count rate based on sequential one minute intervals	Cumulative count rate (counts/min)
0	0	0	0
0·25	4		16·0
0·50	6		12·0
0·75	7		9·0
1·0	17	17	17·0
1·5	17		11·3
2·0	21	4	10·5
3·0	32	11	10·7
4·0	48	16	12·0
5·0	55	7	11·0
6·0	65	10	10·8
7·0	81	16	11·6
8·0	90	9	11·3
9·0	97	7	10·8
10·0	115	18	11·5
11·0	138	23	12·5
12·0	149	11	12·4
13·0	166	17	12·8
14·0	182	16	13·0
15·0	192	10	12·8
16·0	206	14	12·9
17·0	216	10	12·7
18·0	228	12	12·7
19·0	232	4	12·2
20·0	246	14	12·3
21·0	254	8	12·1
22·0	264	10	12·0
23·0	283	19	12·3
24·0	297	14	12·4
25·0	312	15	12·5

Table A.12.

These are the extremes of the range of percentage accuracy.

(2) At $t = 20$ minutes the cumulative count rate is 12·3 per minute. Total counts up to this time are 246 so that the percentage accuracy for this value is

$$\frac{100}{\sqrt{246}} = 6·4\%$$

After 5 minutes the total count is 55, the cumulative count rate is 11 per minute and the percentage accuracy is

$$\frac{100}{\sqrt{55}} = 13·4\%$$

After 10 minutes the total count is 115, the cumulative count rate is 11·5 per minute and the percentage accuracy is

$$\frac{100}{\sqrt{115}} = 9·3\%$$

After 15 minutes the total count is 192, the cumulative count rate is 12·8 per minute and the percentage accuracy is

$$\frac{100}{\sqrt{192}} = 7·2\%$$

These figures show the importance of taking a large number of counts when reasonable accuracy is required.

(3) Both graphs show a significant change at $t = 10$ minutes from which we can conclude that a change in laboratory conditions occured then.

(4) To obtain the count rate of 30 per minute 60 counts were recorded. This gives an accuracy of

$$\frac{100}{\sqrt{60}} = 12.9\%$$

To obtain 60 counts at the background rate would probably take 5 minutes but we cannot be sure of getting 60 counts in this time because of the random nature of the radioactive decay processes.

Test thirteen

The graph of $\log_{10}$ (count rate) against ρx for the various absorbers is shown in Fig. A.13.

(1) Writing the equation as,

$$\log_{10} R = -\frac{c}{2.3} \rho x + \log_{10} R_0$$

we see that this has the form $y = mx + c$ where the slope $= -c/2.3$. Part of the graph shown in Fig. A.13 is a straight line with a negative slope and an intercept on the $\log_{10} R$ axis. We can conclude that the form of the equation is verified if ρx is less than 750 mg cm^{-2}.

Fig. A.13 β Absorption.

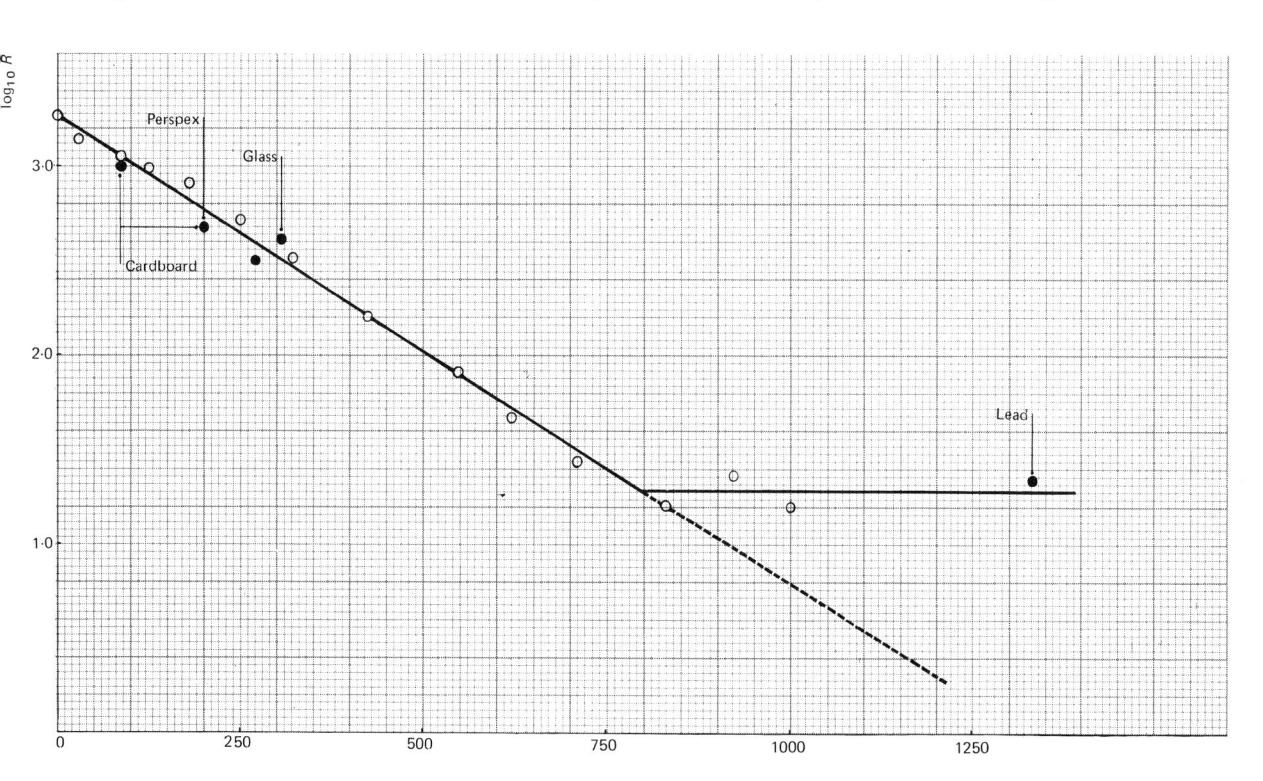

(2) Fairly obviously at 20 counts per minute ($\log_{10} R = 1\cdot 3$) we have reached the background count level. No further reduction in count rate can be produced by use of thicker absorbers. Under these conditions removal of the β source will not produce any effect on the count rate.

(3) The five points for materials other than aluminium are shown on the graph. The point for lead gives a background count value but the others fit onto the aluminium graph quite well. We may tentatively conclude that points for any absorber would lie on this line and that c is a constant with the same value for all materials for this particular β source. To give this conclusion a solid scientific backing many more points for a wide variety of materials with a wide range of ρx values would have to be plotted.

(4) (a) $\log_{10}$ (100 per minute) $= 2\cdot 000$. At $\log_{10} R = 2\cdot 000$ the value of ρx is 515 mg cm^{-2}. The thickness of glass required to give this count rate is

$$x = \frac{515 \times 10^{-3}}{2\cdot 90} = 0\cdot 178 \text{ cm } (1\cdot 78 \times 10^{-3} \text{ m})$$

(b) For lead the equivalent thickness will be

$$x = \frac{515 \times 10^{-3}}{11\cdot 34} = 0\cdot 0454 \text{ cm } (4\cdot 54 \times 10^{-4} \text{ m})$$

(c) The zero thickness count rate has a $\log_{10}$ of $3\cdot 257$. The $\log_{10}$ of half this rate will be $3\cdot 257 - \log_{10} 2 = 3\cdot 257 - 0\cdot 301 = 2\cdot 956$. The value of ρx corresponding to $\log_{10} R = 2\cdot 956$ is 125 mg cm^{-2}. The thickness of aluminium to give this count rate is

$$x = \frac{125 \times 10^{-3}}{2\cdot 70} = 0\cdot 0463 \text{ cm } (4\cdot 63 \times 10^{-4} \text{ m})$$

(d) The equivalent thickness of air would be

$$x = \frac{125 \times 10^{-3}}{1\cdot 29 \times 10^{-3}} = 96\cdot 9 \text{ cm } (0\cdot 969 \text{ m})$$

(5) Some extra points would be useful at values of ρx greater than 350 mg cm^{-2}. You will notice that the experimenter used the same two minute interval for all his counts. This means that the accuracy for large values of ρx is much lower than for the small values. An improvement might be to time the same number of counts for each ρx value used. Is this really practical at count rates near background? Do a few calculations and discuss them with your teacher.

(6) If the new source had the same activity but emitted higher average energy β's the zero thickness value R_0 would still be the same. The fact that the β's are more energetic means that greater thicknesses of material are needed to reduce the count rate to a particular level (β's are more penetrating). Hence the new graph of $\log_{10} R$ against ρx would have the same value of R_0 but larger values of ρx at any given value of $\log_{10} R$. That is, it would have a smaller slope and the constant c would be smaller.

(7) The calculations in the answers to Question 4 showed that the required thickness of absorber

$$= \frac{\text{constant} \times \text{a chosen value of } \log_{10} \text{ count rate}}{\text{density of absorber}}$$

Therefore $\dfrac{\text{thickness of lead}}{\text{equivalent thickness of concrete}}$

$$= \frac{\text{density of concrete}}{\text{density of lead}} = \frac{2 \cdot 20}{11 \cdot 34} = \frac{1}{5 \cdot 16}$$

That is 5·16 times as much concrete as lead is required to provide equivalent shielding. In the storage problem mentioned the 1·0 m of concrete will obviously be preferable to 0·1 m of lead as the thickness ratio is 10:1.

Test fourteen

The values of AB^2 and h are given in Table A.14 and Fig. A.14 shows the graph of AB^2 and h. The slope is CA and equal to 3·52 m.

AB^2, (m²)	h, (m)
0·35	0·1
1·06	0·3
1·74	0·5
2·50	0·7
3·17	0·9
3·84	1·1
4·54	1·3

Table A.14.

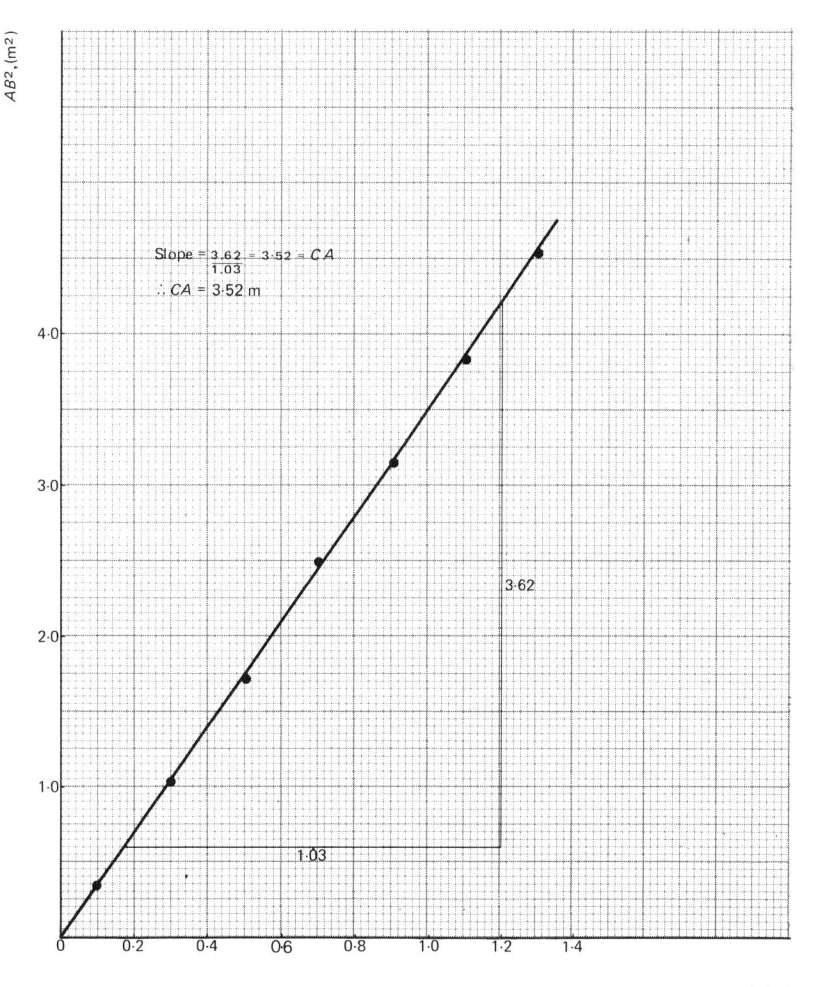

Fig. A.14 Graph of AB^2 against h.

(1) Since the extrapolation to the vertical has been made from the results for a sphere rolling down inclined planes the value of CA will represent the distance *rolled* from rest down a vertical plane in one second and *not* the distance of free fall, as assumed in Galileo's theory.

(2) From Fig. 4.14 it can be shown that when $\alpha = 90°$, $h = AB = AC$. From the graph of AB^2 against h we could find the value of h at which $h^2 = AB^2$ and this value of h would be the value of CA. We know that $CA = 3.52$ m so that the value of AB^2 when $h = 3.52$ m is 12.39 m². Clearly to obtain this value for AB^2 from the graph a long extrapolation would be required and this would not be as accurate as obtaining CA from the slope.

(3) In working out a valid theory we have to take into account the effects of rotation of the sphere. The rotational kinetic energy of a body rotating with angular velocity is $\frac{1}{2}I\omega^2$ where I is its moment of inertia about the axis of rotation. For a solid sphere the moment of inertia about a diameter is $\frac{2}{5}ma^2$ where a is the sphere radius. Therefore the rotational kinetic energy of the rolling sphere is,

$$\tfrac{1}{2}I\omega^2 = \tfrac{1}{2}(\tfrac{2}{5}ma^2)\omega^2 = \tfrac{1}{5}mv^2$$

where v is the linear velocity of the sphere and equal to $a\omega$. Equating the loss in potential energy in rolling the vertical distance CA to the total gain in kinetic energy we obtain,

$$mg \cdot CA = \tfrac{1}{2}mv^2 + \tfrac{1}{5}mv^2$$

Therefore $\quad mg \cdot CA = \dfrac{7}{10}mv^2 \quad$ and $\quad CA = \dfrac{7v^2}{10g}$

The average velocity $\bar{v} = \dfrac{v}{2} = \dfrac{CA}{1}\quad$ so that $\quad v = 2CA$

Therefore $\quad CA = \dfrac{7 \times 4CA^2}{10g}\quad$ and $\quad CA = \dfrac{g}{2.8} = 3.5$ m

(4) It has been shown in the answer to question 3 that the total gain in kinetic energy of the rolling solid sphere is $\frac{7}{10}mv^2$. For the thin hollow sphere of greater radius a_1 and having the same mass m the moment of inertia about a diameter is $\frac{2}{3}ma_1^2$ so that the total gain in kinetic energy is given by,

$$\tfrac{1}{2}(\tfrac{2}{3}ma_1^2)\omega_1^2 + \tfrac{1}{2}mv_1^2$$

where ω_1 and v_1 are the respective angular and linear velocities. Since $v_1 = a_1\omega_1$ the total kinetic energy is

$$\tfrac{1}{3}mv_1^2 + \tfrac{1}{2}mv_1^2 = \tfrac{5}{6}mv_1^2.$$

If the two spheres experience identical losses in potential energy then their gains in kinetic energy must be the same so that, $\frac{7}{10}mv^2 = \frac{5}{6}mv_1^2$. Therefore $v^2 = \frac{50}{42}v_1^2$. Therefore the linear velocity of the solid sphere is greater than that of the hollow sphere and hence the distance BA travelled in one second by the hollow sphere would be less than the distance travelled by the solid sphere.

Test fifteen

Log$_{10}$ W	Log$_{10}$ R
1·398	0
1·813	0·188
0·057	0·295
0·225	0·395
0·367	0·430
0·477	0·477
0·574	0·515
0·659	0·545
0·803	0·596
0·914	0·642
1·015	0·675
1·101	0·705
1·177	0·731
1·248	0·752
1·309	0·774
1·367	0·791
1·422	0·807
1·468	0·824
1·515	0·838
1·561	0·847
1·599	0·862
1·641	0·870

Table A.15.

Table A.15 shows the values of $\log_{10} W$ and $\log_{10} R$ and the graph of $\log_{10} W$ against $\log_{10} R$ has been plotted in Fig. A.15. True origins have been used so that the intercepts can be measured rather than calculated. The tangents to the curve at $W = 24$ W and 38 W ($\log_{10} W = 1·38$ and $1·58$) have been drawn using the plane mirror method mentioned on pages 34 and 35. The slopes of these tangents are similar, so that the values of $\log_{10} K$ obtained are also quite close. However to get K these intercepts must be anti-logged and this will give them very different values. Slight errors in drawing the tangents will therefore produce quite large errors in K, so do not expect to get exactly the values shown in Fig. A.15. From the graph at $W = 24$ W we get a slope of $3·23$ and an intercept of $\bar{2}·81$ so that $n = 3·23$ and $K = 0·0646$. Hence $W = 0·0646 R^{3·23}$ at this point. At $W = 38$ W the slope is $3·39$ and the intercept is $\bar{2}·68$ so that $n = 3·39$ and $K = 0·0479$. Hence $W = 0·0479 R^{3·39}$ at this point.

(1) The assumptions in the theory are:
   (a) energy is only lost from the filament by radiation
   (b) the temperature of the filament is well above room temperature
   (c) the resistance temperature relationship for the filament is linear

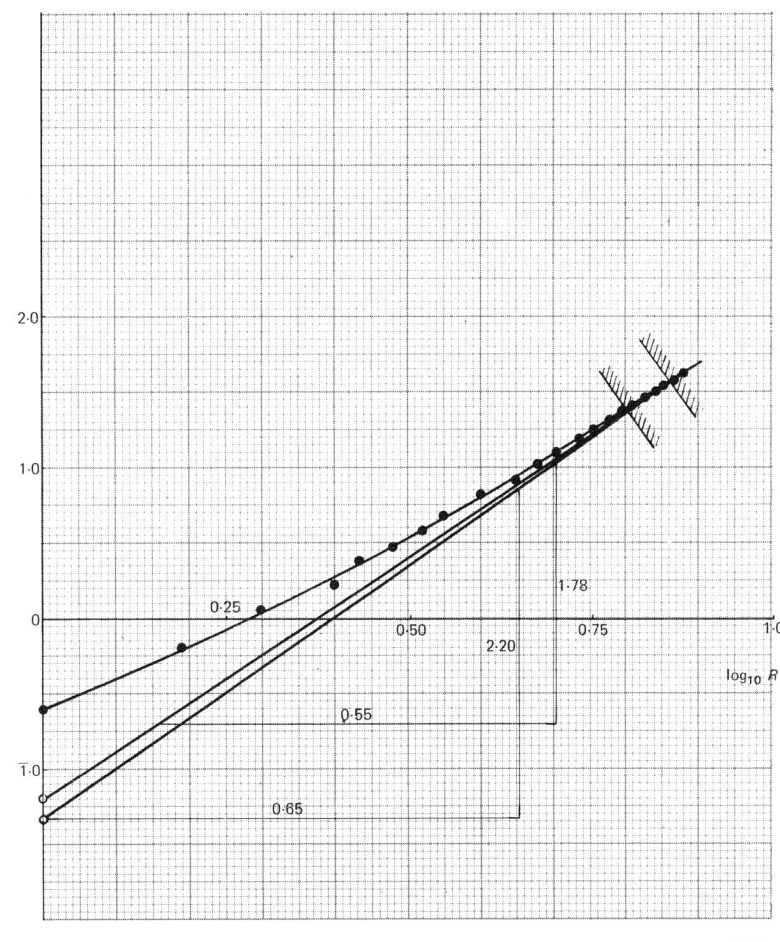

Fig. A.15 Log$_{10}$ W against log$_{10}$ R.

Considering (a), there are clearly considerably losses by conduction through the leads to the filament. We would expect these to be greatest at the higher temperatures.

Considering (b), we would expect the assumption to be invalid at the lower power levels though it is not clear just where it begins to be justified unless we do some calculations which assume a knowledge of the filament operating temperature.

Considering (c), the resistance temperature relationship for most metals is only linear over a limited temperature range and is a shallow curve over the sort of temperature range (300 K to 2000 K) which we are dealing with here. It is difficult to predict how the three assumptions would affect the final validity of the theory but the graph does show an increasing slope as W (and hence temperature) rises. The slope at the upper end is approaching the theoretical value of 4 so we can conclude that the validity of the theory shows overall improvement at the higher temperatures.

(2) Using $K = SA \left(\dfrac{T_A}{R_A}\right)^n$ we solve for SA in each case.

At $W = 24$ W $K = 0\cdot0646 = SA \left(\dfrac{300}{1}\right)^{3\cdot23}$ giving $SA = 0\cdot0646/300^{3\cdot23}$

At $W = 38$ W $K = 0\cdot0479 = SA \left(\dfrac{300}{1}\right)^{3\cdot39}$ giving $SA = 0\cdot0479/300^{3\cdot39}$

Then using $W = SAT^n$

at $W = 24$ W, $24 = \dfrac{0\cdot0646}{300^{3\cdot23}} \cdot T^{3\cdot23}$ giving $T = 1875$ K

at $W = 38$ W, $38 = \dfrac{0\cdot0479}{300^{3\cdot39}} \cdot T^{3\cdot39}$ giving $T = 2140$ K

(3) The value $T = 1875\ K$ at $W = 24$ W is fairly near the expected value so that we can place a fair amount of confidence in the value of 2140 K for the temperature at $W = 38$ W.

(4) The description of the experimental procedure shows that the results were taken over a period of only ten minutes and that the voltage was increased steadily up to the peak value of 18 V. The filament stood up to the over running since (a) it was only used at 44 W for a few minutes at most and (b) it was taken to this power in small steps so that it was not subjected to thermal shock (sudden changes of temperature which cause sudden expansion or contraction of the filament and possible failure).

(5) A car headlamp bulb mounted in a car could not be over run in the way described above. It is subjected to thermal shock when switched on or off, is used for long periods and is also subjected to prolonged vibration which the bench mounted lamp is not.

Test sixteen

(1) The graph of v_t against d^2 is shown in Fig. A.16. A terminal velocity of $350\cdot0$ mm s^{-1} over a distance of $0\cdot8$ m would involve measuring a fall time of $2\cdot3$ s. With a reaction time of $0\cdot2$ s the observer could

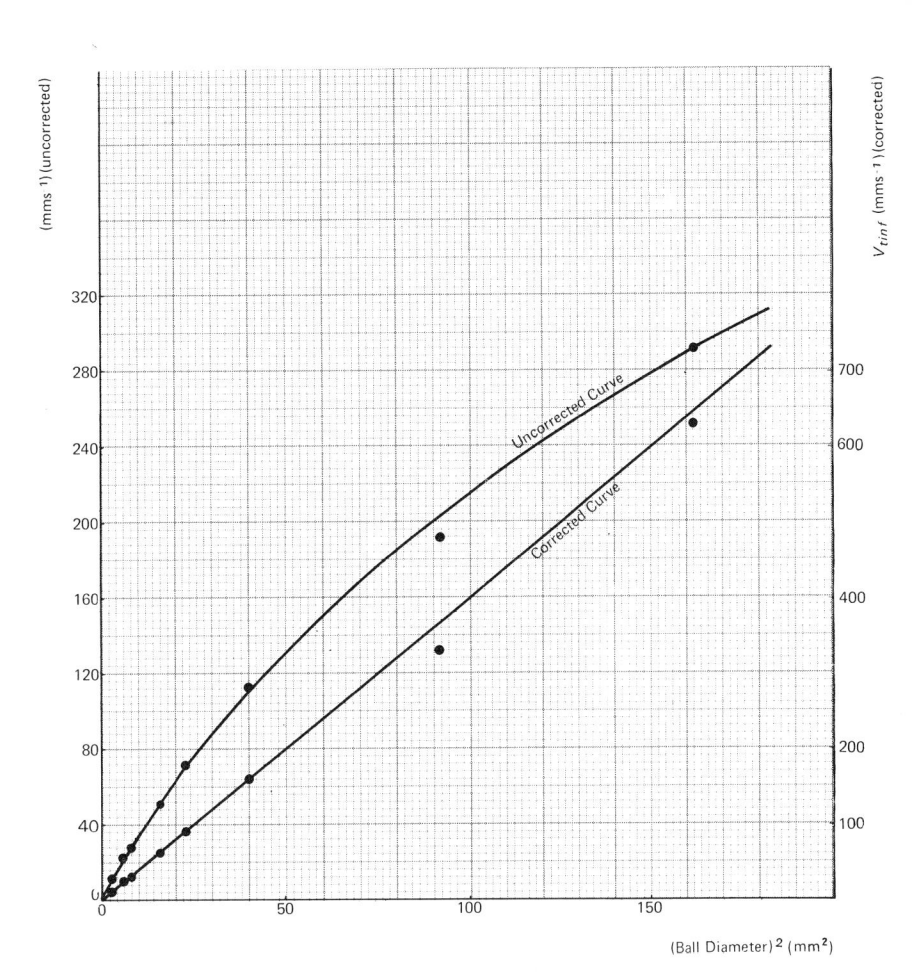

Fig. A.16 Graphs of v_{tm} against (ball diameter)^2 and v_{tinf} against (ball diameter)^2.

obtain a worst possible error of ± 0.4 s. That is approximately 17% error. This is large but the main reason for abandoning the last three readings is that they all appear to have the same measured value of v_t. This makes them suspect.

(2) If you have drawn your graph with care you will find that it is a very shallow curve over the whole of its range. However it is roughly linear for the first four points. Figure A.16 shows this. At the higher velocities the measured values v_{tm} are well below what we would expect if $v_t \propto d^2$ held over the whole range of results.

$\begin{bmatrix}\text{Ball}\\\text{diameter}\end{bmatrix}^2$ d^2, (mm)^2	Uncorrected terminal velocity v_{tm}, (mm s^{-1})	$\dfrac{d}{D}$	$\left(\dfrac{d}{D}\right)^3$	$v_{tinf} = \dfrac{v_{tm}}{\left(1 - 2.104\dfrac{d}{D}\right)}$	$v_{tinf} = \dfrac{v_{tm}}{\left[1 - 2.104\dfrac{d}{D} + 2.09\left(\dfrac{d}{D}\right)^3\right]}$
2.4	9.5	3.35×10^{-2}	3.75×10^{-5}	10.24 mm s^{-1}	
5.7	20.8	5.17×10^{-2}	1.38×10^{-4}	23.30	
10.1	35.0	6.91×10^{-2}	3.30×10^{-4}	40.90	
15.8	50.3	8.63×10^{-2}	6.43×10^{-4}	61.40	
22.7	71.0	10.34×10^{-2}	11.50×10^{-4}		90.40 mm s^{-1}
40.3	114.3	13.80×10^{-2}	26.20×10^{-4}		160.0
91.8	194.5	20.65×10^{-2}	88.50×10^{-4}		333.0
162.0	291.0	27.60×10^{-2}	208.0×10^{-4}		529.0

Table A.16.

(3) The corrected results are shown in Table A.16 and plotted on the same graph as the uncorrected ones but to a different scale which is shown on the right hand side. Such double scales are quite frequently met in advanced work. The corrected graph is a good straight line up to $v_{tinf} = 162.0$ mm s^{-1}. Above that the points become very scattered but there are not enough of them to draw a valid general conclusion. We would however expect a turbulence effect to set in behind the falling ball at the higher velocities and this would have the effect of still further reducing v_t below the expected (corrected) value. This does appear to be the case on our graph.

(4) In the original experiment we have already seen that the results are unreliable at $v_{tm} = 350.0$ mm s^{-1} ($d = 15.88$ mm and above) because of the difficulty of timing the short fall times. If we want to test the full form of the equation using values of d such that $(d/D)^5$ is not negligible we clearly cannot use values of $d > 12.71$ mm. The only way to get d/D large and keep v_{tm} small enough to be measured accurately is to use a much smaller diameter tube. That is reduce D. If d/D has to be 0.95 then with $d = 12.71$ mm D would need to be 13.4 mm. With $d = 12.71$ mm using the original tube $v_{tm} = 291.0$ mm s^{-1} but using a smaller diameter tube will increase the 'wall effect' and the measured velocities v_{tm} will be much less than this (hence the fall times much greater).

(5) The graph of v_{tm} against d^2 shows that v_{tm} levels off as d^2 increases. A little thought will show that as $d \to D$ v_{tm} will in fact *fall*, and if $d = D$ the ball is a perfect fit in the tube and will not fall ($v_{tm} = 0$ in this case).

(6) The correction formula tells us that when $d = D$, $v_{tm} = v_{tinf} \times 0.036$ (obtained by putting $d/D = 1$ into the full form of the correction formula). This is not strictly true since we know that if $d = D$ the ball will not fall, $v_{tm} = 0$ and $v_{tinf} \neq 0$. In fact the full correction equation breaks down at $d = D$. To make it applicable in such a case further terms involving $(d/D)^7$, $(d/D)^9$ and so on would be required. However the equation $v_{tm} = v_{tinf} \times 0.036$ gives us an approximate idea of v_{tm} as $d \to D$. Clearly if d is some moderate value v_{tinf} is a moderate value also and v_{tm} is 0.036 times this moderate value. v_{tm} is very small and v_{tinf} moderate not v_{tm} moderate and v_{tinf} huge.

(7) Forcing an object down a tube containing a liquid when it is a very tight fit in the tube is the principle of the dash pot (hydraulic) damper. This is used on cars, motor cycles, etc to damp down the motion of the body of the vehicle as it oscillates on its springing due to road shocks. The device usually comprises a piston moving in a cylinder of hydraulic fluid. The piston is a very tight fit in the cylinder and has a fine hole connecting its front to its back face. As it is forced down the tube the fluid is forced through this hole and provides a large but not infinite resistance to the piston's motion. The same action occurs on the reverse stroke and any oscillation of the piston is rapidly damped out.

(8) We would expect the resistance to motion of the cubes to be greater than for the equivalent spheres. There are two reasons for this:
   (a) a larger surface area is presented by the cube than by the same

volume in a spherical shape hence the viscous resistive force will be greater

(b) the cubes would probably tumble as they fell. This would induce turbulence behind them even at low terminal velocities and so would increase the drag and reduce the terminal velocity

The overall effect would therefore be a reduction in terminal velocity.

Clearly shape has a big influence on terminal velocity and the highest velocities would be obtained with shapes which minimise turbulence and at the same time have the least possible surface area. The shape of the dolphin is a good example of this.

Test seventeen

If d is plotted against $1/\theta$ (θ in radians) a straight line graph is obtained having a slope of a. Figure A.17(a) shows the graphs of d against $1/\theta$ for the two sets of results given in Table A.17(a). $a_1 = 0.4$ mm and $a_2 = 0.6$ mm.

(1) Using the calibration curve of d against θ shown in Fig. A.17(b) θ has the value of $2.3°$ when $d = 10$ mm.

(2) This method is unsuitable for measuring very small angles because as θ approaches zero d approaches infinity, and the fringes become less distinct as the fringe separation increases. The equation $d = a/\theta$ has been obtained from the equation

$$d = \frac{a}{2 \sin \theta/2}$$

by making the approximation $\sin \theta/2 = \theta/2$ for small angles. This approximation only holds for angles less than about $10°$.

Grating spacings = a_1		Grating spacings = a_2	
d, (mm)	$1/\theta$, (rad^{-1})	d, (mm)	$1/\theta$, (rad^{-1})
22.9	57.14	34.3	57.14
11.5	28.65	17.2	28.65
7.6	19.08	11.4	19.08
5.7	14.33	8.6	14.33
4.6	11.45	6.9	11.45
3.8	9.62	5.8	9.62

Table A.17(a).

Fig. A.17(a) Graphs of d against $1/\theta$.

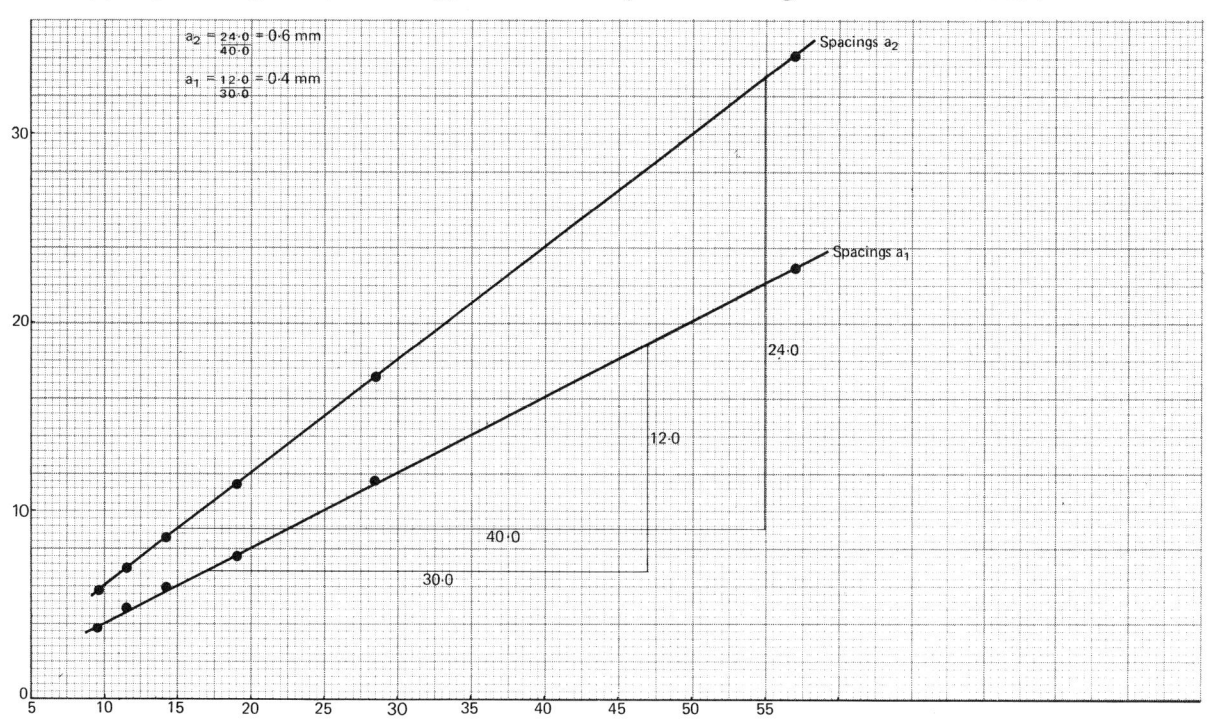

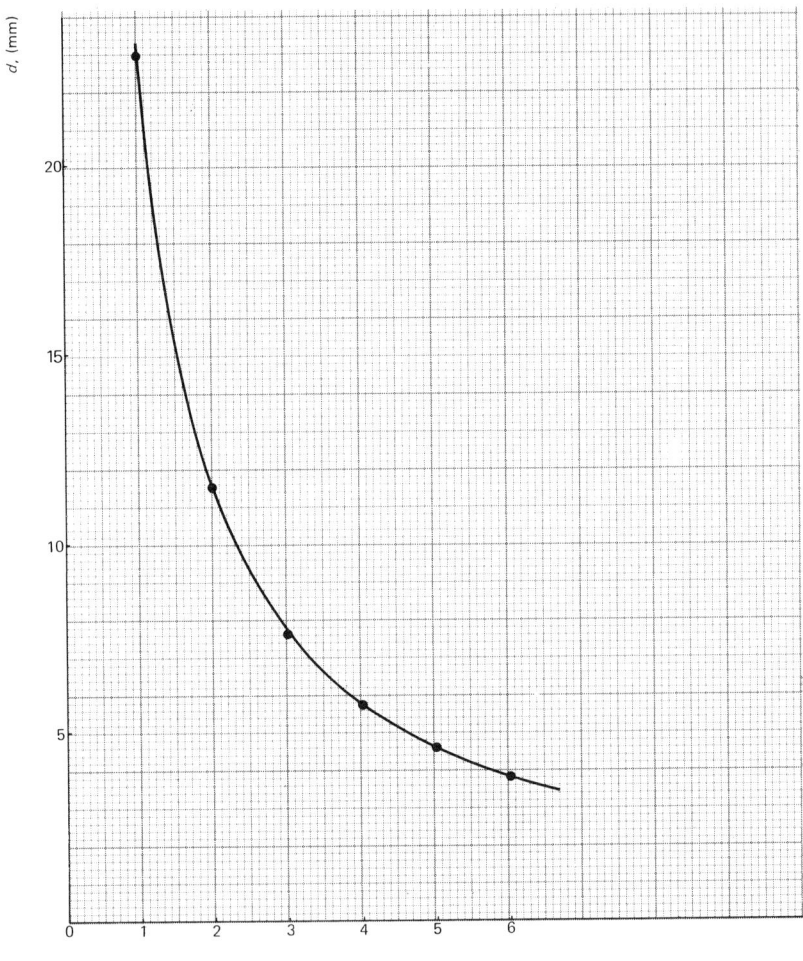

Fig. A.17(b) Graph of d against θ for gratings of spacing a_1.

θ, (degrees)

The calculated values of d for various values of θ for the unequal pair of gratings are given in Table A.17(b) and the graph of d against θ is shown in Fig. A.17(c).

(3) The largest increase in the fringe spacing for an increase in the value of θ of 3° is 0·06 mm. This holds for anywhere between about 9° and 30° since the graph is approximately linear in this region. Hence this pair of gratings is unsuitable for measuring angular changes of 3° or less when using a travelling microscope having an accuracy of ±0·05 mm.

(4) If $a_1 = a_2 = a$ then

$$d = \frac{a^2}{\sqrt{2a^2(1-\cos\theta)}} = \frac{a}{\sqrt{2(1-\cos\theta)}}$$

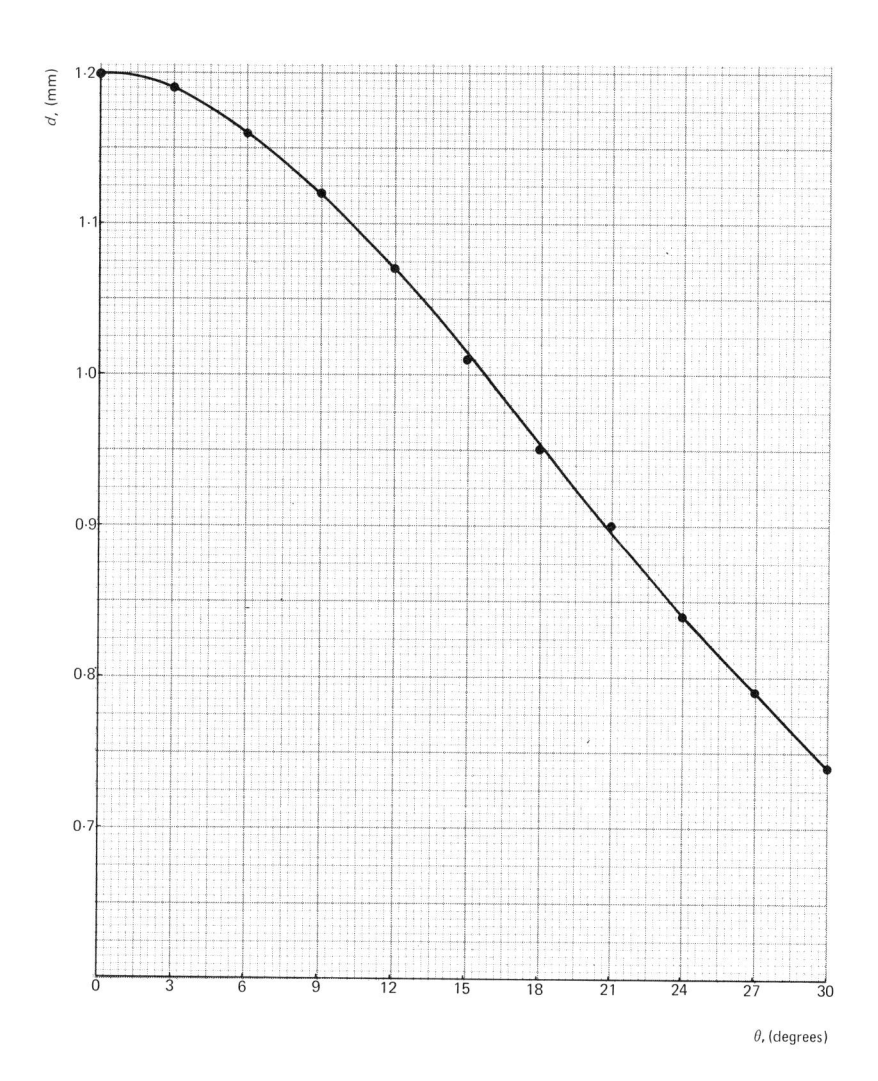

Fig. A.17(c) Graph of d against θ for unequal gratings.

Table A.17(b).

d, (mm)	θ, (degrees)
1·20	0
1·19	3
1·16	6
1·12	9
1·07	12
1·01	15
0·95	18
0·90	21
0·84	24
0·79	27
0·74	30

Since $\cos = 1 - 2\sin^2 \theta/2$ it follows that

$$2(1 - \cos \theta) = 4\sin^2 \frac{\theta}{2}$$

Therefore

$$d = \frac{a}{2 \sin \theta/2}$$

(5) When in contact the spacings of the two gratings subtend the same angles at the eye and therefore their apparent sizes are the same. However when the upper one is raised its spacings subtend a larger angle at the eye so that the spacings appear larger than those of the lower grating and the resultant moiré pattern is that which would be obtained with two unequal gratings.

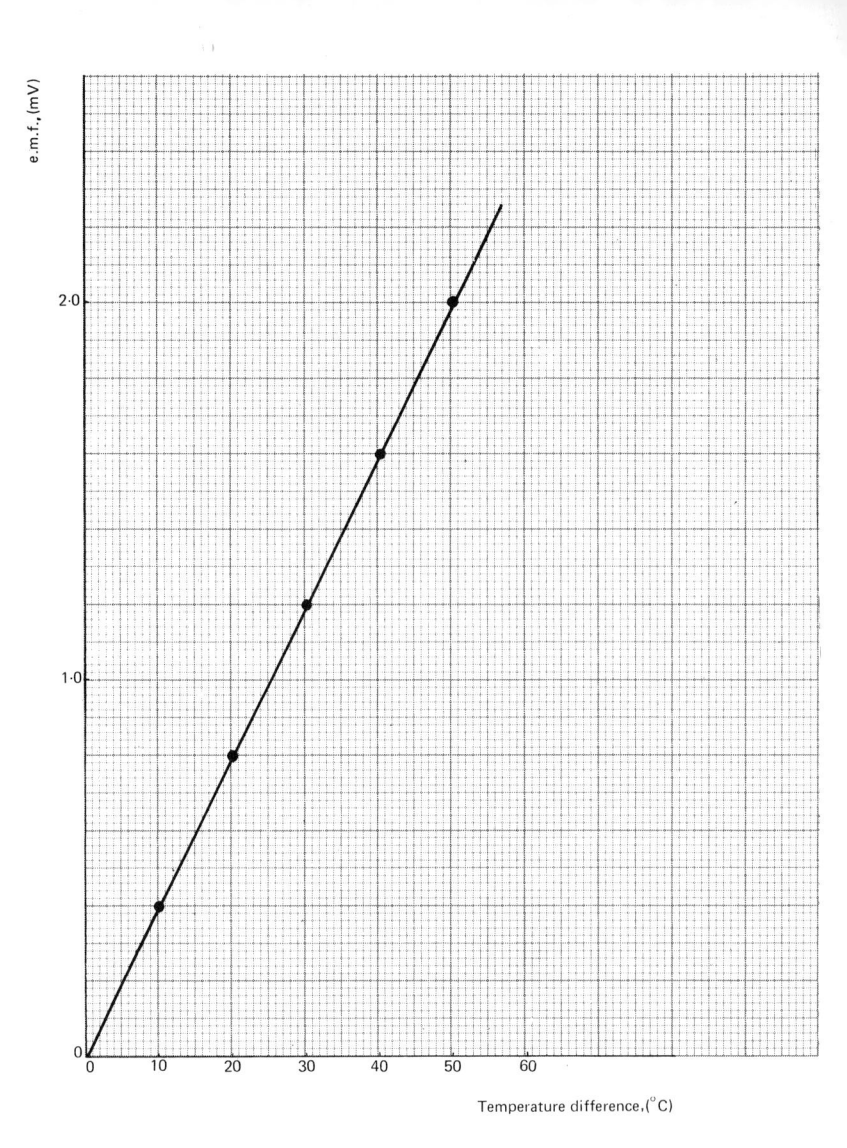

Fig. A.18(a) Calibration graph for thermocouple.

Test eighteen

(1) *A* and *B* clearly do not have exactly the same view of the sky since their shielding strips are differently orientated with respect to the sun. However the scattered 'sky' radiation does fall on them roughly equally from all directions so that their view of this radiation is the same, as is required by the theory.

The foil strip in front of *B* shields it from the direct solar radiation but also from some of the 'sky' radiation. To make sure that *A* has the same amount of 'sky' radiation but is always fully exposed to the direct solar radiation its foil strip is identical to that of *B* but is positioned 90° further round the cylinder. The waste pipe runs in front of the foil shield for *B* so as not to affect the shielding of either sphere.

(2) The approach of the observer to the device might (particularly in strong sunlight) cause a difference in the 'sky' radiation falling on each couple junction. For example if he approached so that *A* was shielded from him *B* might pick up a little scattered radiation from him and so give a false (too low) reading on the millivoltmeter. Remote observation

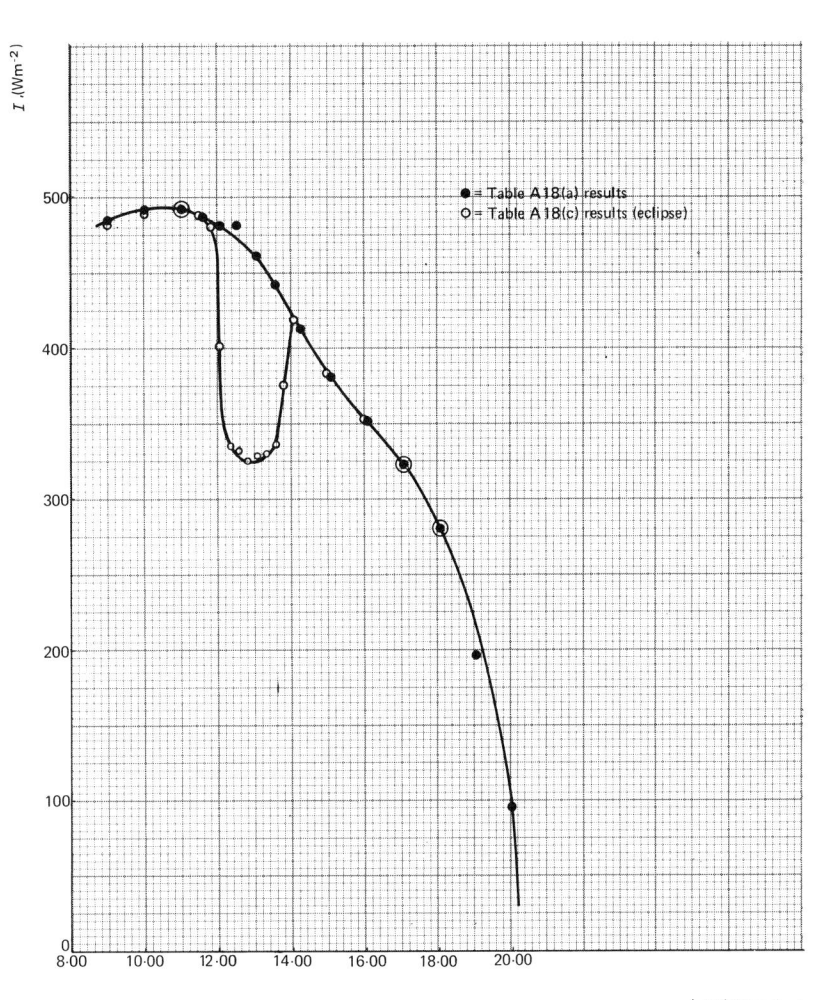

Fig. A.18(b).
⊙ = Table A.18(a) results
△ = Table 4.18(c) results (eclipse)

would eliminate this possibility and also that of shadowing the device when taking a reading.

(3) One of the advantages of the thermocouple for temperature measurement is its small size and consequent rapid response to changing temperature. If the couple junctions were encased in large spheres this advantage would be lost. Also if the spheres were of 2 cm diameter they would be almost touching and re-radiation from A would strongly affect B (in the theory it is assumed that the spheres do not 'see' each other at all). A large sphere B would also be difficult to shield without using very wide foil strips which in turn would cause unwanted shadowing of A.

(4) The exposed sphere A will lose energy by radiation but also by conduction down the leads (a similar situation to that of the heated filament in Test 15). Sphere B which is only exposed to 'sky' radiation will be at T_2 which is only slightly above T_B. We would not expect much heat loss by conduction down into the base (which is at T_B)

Local time (hrs)	E.m.f. (mV)	Temp. difference (T_1-T_2), (°C)	I (Wm^{-2})
9·00	0·89	22·4	482
10·03	9·00	22·7	488
11·00	9·00	22·7	488
11·34	0·89	22·5	484
12·02	0·88	22·3	480
12·31	0·88	22·3	480
13·00	0·85	21·3	459
13·28	0·82	20·6	443
14·05	0·76	19·1	412
15·01	0·70	17·6	379
16·04	0·64	16·2	349
17·01	0·59	15·0	323
18·00	0·52	13·1	282
19·00	0·36	9·0	194
20·00	0·18	4·4	95

Table A.18.

from B. But A, which may reach 23°C above T_2, will have greater conduction losses due to the greater thermal gradients involved (some heat also flows from A to B by conduction).

The overall effect of the conduction losses is to reduce both T_1 and T_2 and to reduce their difference (T_1-T_2). Therefore the millivoltmeter readings will be slightly lower than we might expect on the basis of the theory. We may neglect the conduction and convection effects in the air surrounding A and B.

The calibration graph for the copper constantan thermocouple is shown in Fig. A.18(a). The values of I throughout the day are shown in Table A.18 and plotted in Fig. A.18(b).

(5) (a) Since A is a sphere it ought to receive $\pi r^2 S$ watts at any angle of elevation of the sun. All the values of I on the graph should therefore be the same and equal to S. This would be true in the absence of atmospheric absorption. In fact the atmosphere quite strongly absorbs and scatters a great deal of the incident solar radiation (particularly in the ultra-violet part of the spectrum).

(b) Part of the apparent variation of I throughout the day is due to the variation of the effective thickness of the atmosphere through which the solar radiation has to pass to reach the recorder. Obviously the effective thickness is greatest at dawn and dusk.

(c) If we define the absorption factor as

$$\left(\frac{S-I_{\max}}{S}\right)100\%$$

that is, the ratio of the absorbed radiation to the incident we obtain,

$$\text{absorbtion factor} = \left(\frac{1387-492}{1387}\right)100 = \frac{895\times 100}{1387} = 64.6\%$$

(6) The total direct energy received per square metre in a given time will be the sum of all the $I\times t$ products in that time. That is, the area under the I against time graph. This is explained on pages 25 to 28. To find the total energy received by sphere A we take the area under the curve between 9.00 hours and 18.00 hours and multiply this by the effective absorbing area of A (πr^2). Using 25 W m$^{-2}\times 1$ hr squares for counting we obtain a total of 154 squares each representing 25 W hr m^{-2} = 25×3600 J m^{-2}. $\pi r^2 = \pi \times 10^{-6}$ m^2. Therefore the total energy received = $154\times 25\times \pi \times 10^{-6}\times 3600 = 43.6$ J.

(7) We might expect the value of I to be greatest at the local noon value when the effective thickness of the atmosphere is least. In fact I is fairly constant up to 12.00 hours and then drops sharply. The curve is not symmetrical about 12.00 hours. The main reason for this is thought to be the build up of dust and water vapour in the atmosphere during the day due to convection currents. There is an appreciable lag between the increase of I after dawn and the rise of temperature of the earth's surface so that the dust raising convection currents do not set in strongly until after mid-day.

(8) By superimposing the eclipse recording onto that taken a few days previously as shown in Fig. A.18(b) we can see that the eclipse began at approximately 11.30 hours and ended at 14.00 hours. In fact it

would probably be more accurate to observe and time the eclipse by eye rather than use the graph.

(9) The minimum value of I during the eclipse is 326 W m^{-2} and the normal corresponding value of I is 467 W m^{-2}. If we assume that I is proportional to the effective area of the sun's disc the maximum area covered will be,

$$\left(\frac{467-326}{467}\right) 100 = 30\%$$

Fig. A.18(c) Campbell-Stokes recorder.

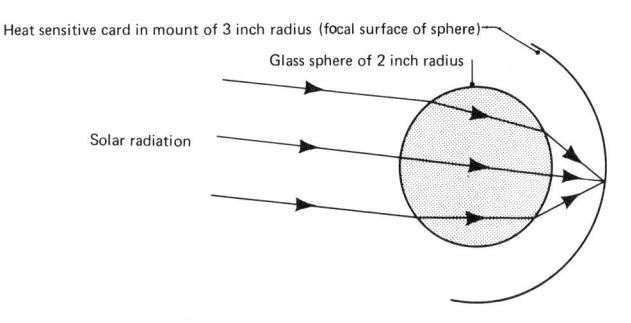

(10) The layout of the Campbell–Stokes recorder is shown in Fig. A.18(c). The student's design is not really a replacement for the Campbell–Stokes type at seaside resorts since it requires fairly skilled handling, has moving parts and provides a full record of the solar intensity. The Campbell–Stokes provides only a sun/no sun record which is all that is required at a seaside resort for publicity purposes and has the great advantage of having no moving parts.

Test nineteen

Table A.19 gives the values of f and $1/b^2$, and these results have been plotted in Fig. A.19(a). The value of the Young's Modulus of the glass is $7 \cdot 05 \times 10^{10}$ Nm^{-2}.

(1) When b is very large $1/b^2$ is very small and can be neglected with respect to $1/a^2$. Therefore the equation for the fundamental frequency becomes,

$$f = \frac{h\pi}{4\sqrt{3}} \left[\frac{1}{a^2}\right] \left[\frac{Eg}{\rho(1-v^2)}\right]^{\frac{1}{2}}$$

This frequency corresponds to the intercept on the f axis on your graph. If $a = 0 \cdot 1$ m the above equation gives a value of 3806 Hz (note that this value could be obtained by measuring the intercept for $a = 1 \cdot 0$ m and multiplying it by 100 which is the ratio of $0 \cdot 1^2$ to $1 \cdot 0^2$).

(2) As b tends to zero $1/b^2$ tends to infinity so that the fundamental frequency approaches infinity also. The graph being a straight line of positive slope confirms this.

(3) The fundamental frequency of this window is 154·6 Hz. We would expect the fundamental frequency of the church window to be much lower than for a single large pane. The fact that it is jointed increases its flexibility and so reduces its effective value of Young's Modulus. (Poisson's ratio is hardly affected).

Fig. A.19(a) Graph of f against $1/b^2$.

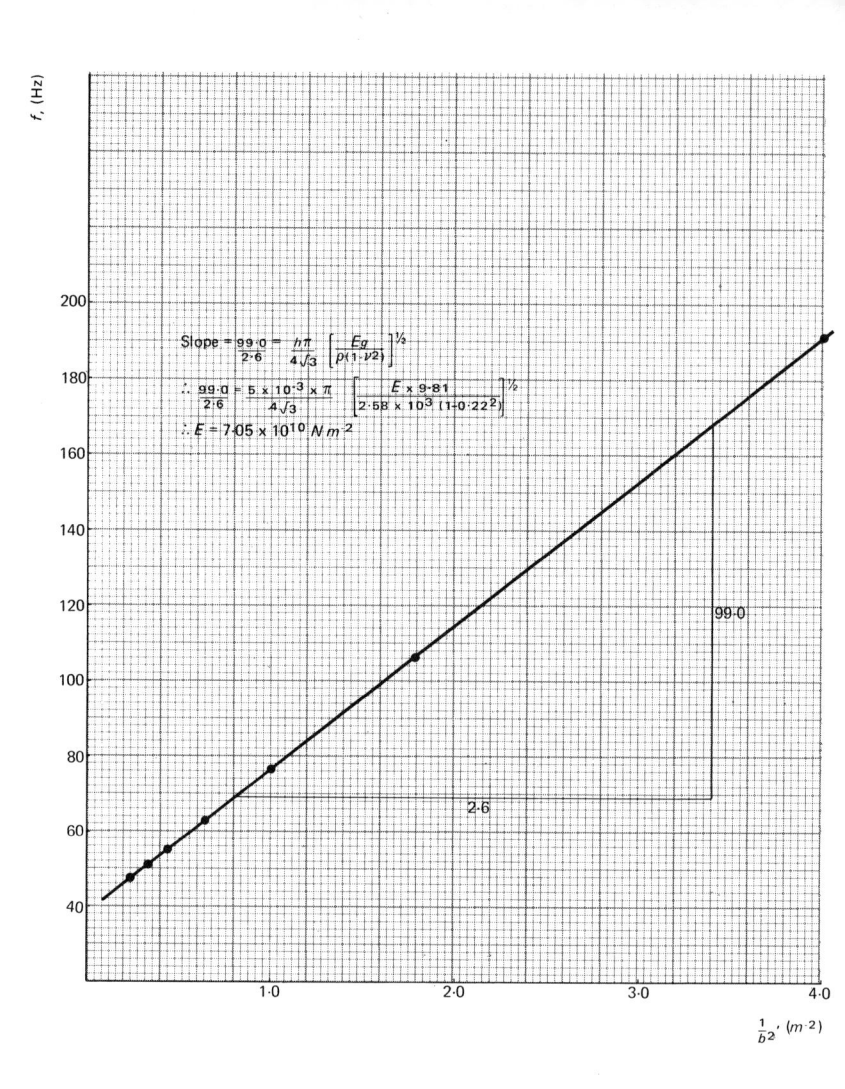

On the graph:
$$\text{Slope} = \frac{99 \cdot 0}{2 \cdot 6} = \frac{h\pi}{4\sqrt{3}} \left[\frac{Eg}{\rho(1-\nu^2)} \right]^{1/2}$$

$$\therefore \frac{99 \cdot 0}{2 \cdot 6} = \frac{5 \times 10^{-3} \times \pi}{4\sqrt{3}} \left[\frac{E \times 9 \cdot 81}{2 \cdot 58 \times 10^3 (1 - 0 \cdot 22^2)} \right]^{1/2}$$

$$\therefore E = 7 \cdot 05 \times 10^{10} \, N \, m^{-2}$$

f, (Hz)	$1/b^2$, (m^{-2})
191·4	4·00
106·4	1·78
76·6	1·00
62·8	0·64
55·1	0·44
50·9	0·33
47·9	0·25

Table A.19.

(4) Since the edges of the window are supported they must be nodal lines. The values of M and N tell us how many half wavelengths there are in each dimension and enable us to locate the other nodal positions. The different cases are shown in Fig. A.19(b).

(5) The total energy of a system oscillating with simple harmonic motion is $\frac{1}{2}ma^2\omega^2$ where m is the mass, a the amplitude and ω the angular frequency. If the energy of the sonic boom applied to each roof is the same we obtain $\frac{1}{2}m_1a_1^2\omega^2 = \frac{1}{2}m_2a_2^2\omega^2$. Therefore

$$\frac{a_1}{a_2} = \sqrt{\frac{m_2}{m_1}}$$

and although this theory may not apply exactly we would expect the heavier roof (St. David's) to show the smaller amplitude of vibration.

(6) The sonic boom originates along the leading edges of the wing and the tail of an aircraft. Most military aircraft have a separate tail and produce a double boom, the second originating from the tail plane. Concorde having a delta wing form and no separate tail plane produces only a single shock wave. The energy in a supersonic shock wave

Fig. A.19(b).

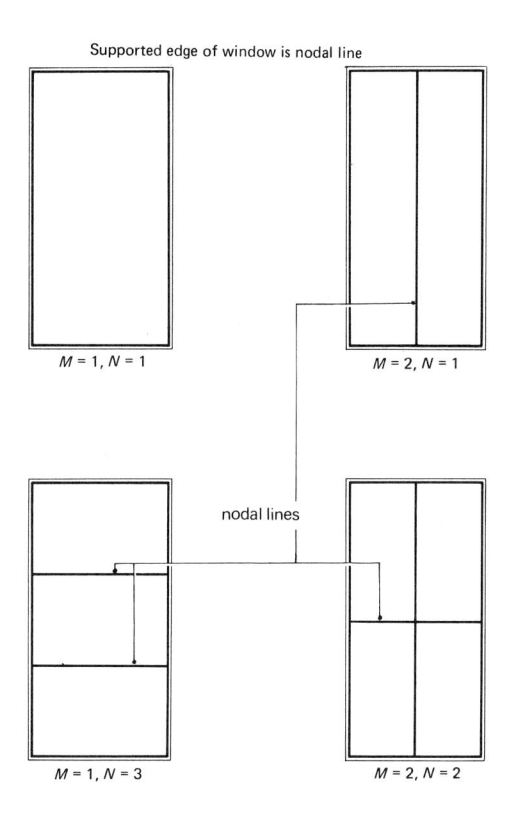

Supported edge of window is nodal line

$M = 1, N = 1$ $M = 2, N = 1$

nodal lines

$M = 1, N = 3$ $M = 2, N = 2$

depends on the mass of the aircraft so that the intensity produced by Concorde is greater than that produced by the smaller military aircraft.

Test twenty

The results of Table 4.20 are shown plotted in Fig. A.20. Although you were only asked to plot the positive values of R the negative values have also been shown to give you an idea of the shape of each curve. The head of each curve is not easy to draw since some of the points on the curves are superimposed.

(1) At $T = 3.5$ s the possible values of R are 0·49 m, 0·62 m, 0·70 m, 0·75 m and 0·77 m. We have to discard the value $R = 0.49$ m since it corresponds to a value of $r = 0.1$ m. The weight bar cannot be above seat level so that r cannot be less than 0·2 m.

(2) Above $T = 5.0$ s the values of R are becoming rather large and the chair would cease to be a practical possibility in its present form. The engineer knew that the period of oscillation of small yachts is somewhere in the range 5 to 10 seconds in rough seas and wondered if with T greater than 5 seconds his chair could produce nausea.

(3) The stability equation $Mgy \cos \theta = wgr \sin \theta$ does not specify forward or backward tilt therefore we would expect the same degree of stability forwards and backwards.

(4) A backward tilt of 20° would probably be acceptable (the back is well supported in this position) but a similar forward tilt would produce an unacceptable feeling of insecurity. The angle of tilt in either direction could be limited by fitting soft buffers or springs to the rolling surfaces.

Fig. A.20 Graph of R against T, where

$$T^2 = \frac{4\pi^2}{g}\left(3\cdot64R^2 + 0\cdot728 + \frac{R^2}{r} - 2R + r\right)$$

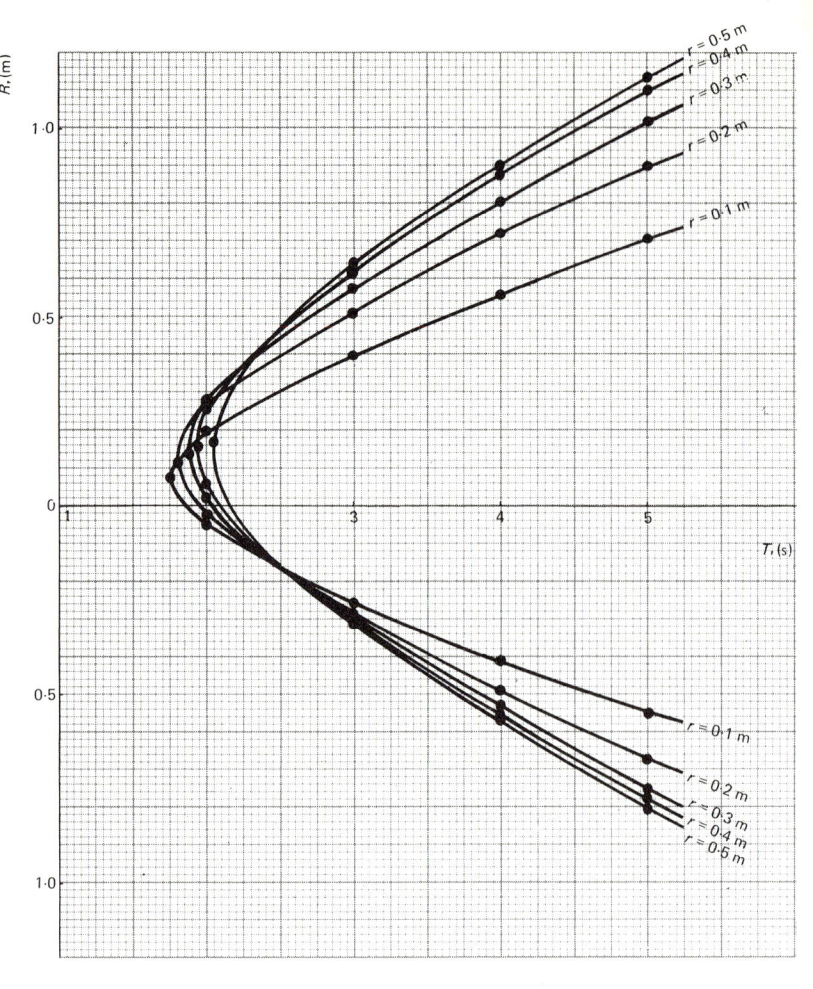

(5) As already mentioned r can only take values of 0·2 m upwards. Using $M/w = 3\cdot64r$ and putting $M = 100$ kg we obtain,

$$w = 137\cdot0 \text{ kg for } r = 0\cdot2 \text{ m}$$
$$w = 90\cdot8 \text{ kg for } r = 0\cdot3 \text{ m}$$
$$w = 62\cdot2 \text{ kg for } r = 0\cdot4 \text{ m}$$
$$w = 54\cdot9 \text{ kg for } r = 0\cdot5 \text{ m}$$

In the answer to (1) we have seen that at $T = 3\cdot5$ s for $r = 0\cdot5$ m ($w = 54\cdot9$ kg) the radius R of the chair is 0·77 m.

(6) Values of R greater than 0·6 m could be used if the length of the seat was reduced and a step or rest provided for the feet at 0·6 m below seat level.

(7) The best set of values is probably $R = 0\cdot77$ m, $w = 54\cdot9$ kg and $r = 0\cdot5$ m. This is the lowest possible stabilising weight bar value and R is not too large. These values would however require the modification in the answer to Question 6.

(8) Putting $R = r$ and $M/w = 3\cdot 64r$ the formula becomes,

$$T^2 = \frac{4\pi^2}{g} \times 3\cdot 64(R^2 + 0\cdot 2)$$

and if $R = 0$ this gives a value of $T = 1\cdot 71$ s. This makes no physical sense. A little thought will show that the period of an infinitely small chair would be indeterminate. The anomaly arises due to putting $R = r = 0$ which gives

$$\frac{(R-r)^2}{r} = \frac{0}{0}$$

which is indeterminate, not zero as you have previously assumed. That is, $(R-r)$ can be zero and

$$\frac{(R-r)^2}{r} = 0$$

provided $r \neq 0$. If $r = 0$ also the quotient is indeterminate.

(9) From the engineer's point of view the chair is interesting in that it is simple and would be easy to produce (fibre glass mouldings) and assemble. Its shape would blend with other modern fittings quite well. From the housewife's angle however it looks very different. Its weight of approximately 60 kg would make it very difficult to move for cleaning and it would not have a good effect on the carpet when in use. If carpets were not used it would probably produce a rumble when oscillating.